WRITINGS OF
EDITH STEIN

Edith Stein (Sister Benedicta of the Cross).

WRITINGS OF
EDITH STEIN

*Selected, translated
and introduced by*
HILDA GRAEF

THE NEWMAN PRESS
Westminster, Maryland
1956

Nihil Obstat Daniel Duivesteijn, S.T.D.
Censor deputatus

Imprimatur E. Morrogh Bernard
Vic. Gen.

Westmonasterii, die 23a Martii, 1956

Library of Congress Catalog Card Number: 56—9323

CONTENTS

INTRODUCTION

In recent years the figure of Edith Stein has increasingly captured the imagination of readers not only in her native Germany, but also in many other European countries as well as in Great Britain and the United States. Hers was indeed an unusual fate, yet in many ways symbolic of our age. Born in Breslau (Silesia) in 1891, she was the youngest child of an orthodox Jewish family, brought up in the traditions of her race and religion. Yet, like many other German Jews of that period, she lost her ancestral faith at a very early age, but retained a passionate desire for truth and a high moral idealism that made a deep impression on all who met her. Her remarkable intellectual gifts showed themselves already in her school days, and as a young student she soon immersed herself in philosophical speculation. Among the schools of thought that arose in the years before the First World War one attracted her special attention; this was Edmund Husserl's new method known as phenomenology. Reacting against Neo-Kantianism, Husserl attempted to oust the prevalent idealistic philosophy by going back to the world of objects or 'phenomena' which, in contrast to Kant, he considered knowable. Edith Stein was deeply impressed by his philosophy which she hoped would be able to satisfy her thirst for truth. So, in 1913, she went to Goettingen to study under Husserl. She soon became one of his most brilliant pupils, and, after completing her doctor's thesis on the subject of 'empathy', was for a short time his assistant.

The phenomenological method aimed at examining all departments of human life objectively and in the words of Husserl, without any 'blinkers'. Hence religion, too, was made an object of investigation by many of Husserl's disciples. Edith Stein came into contact with living Christianity for the first time after the death of one of her fellow philosophers, Adolf Reinach, who was killed in the war in November 1917. She had been asked to help his widow to sort out his papers, a task she dreaded, for the Reinachs' marriage had been exceptionally happy, and being very sensitive herself, Edith was afraid of having to face a shattered home and a disconsolate widow. But her hostess had become a Christian, together with her husband, only a year before, and her new religion gave her so much strength that she was able not only to overcome her own deep grief but also to be a source of consolation to others. This experience made a deep impression on Edith and brought her face to face with the power that emanates from the Cross of Christ. A further influence counteracting her agnosticism was the philosopher Max Scheler, whom she had first met in 1913. In 1916 he had become reconciled to the Catholic Church which he had left after marrying a divorced woman, and his inspiring lectures attracted many young German intellectuals to Catholicism.

But it was reserved to St. Teresa of Avila, the great reformer of the Carmelite Order, to break the last resistances of Edith Stein. She tells us herself how one evening, when she was staying in the house of friends, she picked up at random a volume from their bookshelves and took it with her to her room. It was the *Life* of St. Teresa, written by herself. As soon as she had begun to read she was so fascinated by it that she could not lay down the book again, but read on till she had finished it in the small hours of the morning. She finally closed it with the firm conviction that this was the truth and that she had to become a Catholic. She was baptized on New Year's Day, 1922. Naturally her conversion caused intense grief to her devout Jewish mother and the other members of her family, who felt that Edith had broken completely with all they held dear. She did all she could to bridge the gulf that was now separating them from her, but, on their side at least, the relations could never be quite the same as before. Edith herself prayed incessantly for their conversion, but only one of her sisters followed her into the Church.

Soon after her conversion she abandoned her academic career and accepted a post as teacher at a convent school run by Dominican nuns at Speyer. At first she devoted herself entirely to prayer and her school duties; but soon she felt the need to resume her intellectual activities and to make herself acquainted with traditional Catholic philosophy. Though still giving a large part of her time to the recitation of the divine office and to contemplative prayer, as she was to do throughout her life, she now began to study St. Thomas Aquinas. In the beginning she found this far from easy. It was indeed a far cry from the world of modern philosophy to that of medieval Scholasticism. She herself was disconcerted when she first began to study Aquinas, for, according to her own account, she was "constantly troubled by the question: According to what method does he proceed? I had been accustomed to the phenomenological method, which uses no traditional teaching but examines everything that is needed for the solution of a question *ab ovo*. I was baffled by a procedure that adduces sometimes Scriptural passages, sometimes citations from the Fathers, or again sayings of the old philosophers in order to deduce results from them". *(Endliches und Ewiges Sein, p. 489)*. There is no better method of really penetrating into the thought of an author than to translate him, and so Edith Stein undertook the difficult task of rendering St. Thomas' *Quaestiones disputatae de veritate* into German. It was no word-by-word translation, however, but she adapted the work to the needs of modern readers by giving explanations where they were required and smoothing the medieval form of objections, counter-arguments, exposition and refutation of objections into a continuous discussion in the manner of a modern treatise. Despite certain shortcomings pointed out by expert Thomists, the work was given a very favourable reception and established Edith Stein's reputation as a serious Catholic thinker.

Her work as a school teacher also led her to interest herself in questions of feminine education, and she was soon in great demand as a speaker in various teachers' organizations. Though her desire to withdraw from the world and give herself entirely to prayer in Carmel remained undiminished, her spiritual advisers opposed it on the grounds that her work for the Church was too important to be sacrificed for a purely contemplative vocation. In the spring of 1932 she accepted a post as lecturer at the Catholic Educational Institute at Muenster in Westphalia, where she remained till the beginning of 1933.

9

A number of the lectures she gave during this time were collected in a volume entitled *Frauenbildung und Frauenberufe,* four of which are reproduced in this anthology. They show with what deep apprehension she viewed the increasing destruction of family life and the glorification of mere sexuality. "This", she writes in one of these essays, "occupies such a prominent position in science as well as in literature, it is so widely discussed and given such importance in everyday life, that even the children meet it constantly". Though she felt that this was a lamentable state of affairs, she was the last person to shirk unpleasant facts. She saw that the Catholic teaching on marriage as an indissoluble union was the only solid bulwark against the destructive tendencies of modern thought and education, but she realized at the same time that a mere repetition of the Church's teaching was not enough. Hence she advocated a re-examination of the whole complex of sex psychology, sex education and pathology from the Catholic point of view in educational and medical practice as well as in everyday life. She also demanded a more thorough training for women in their political and civic duties, since she knew that at least part of the success of National Socialism was due to the emotional attraction Hitler and his methods had for women, who constituted an appreciable part of the electorate that voted for him.

With Hitler's advent to power in January 1933 her educational career came to an end, since the Nazi régime tolerated no 'non-Aryans'. She felt that she was at last free to gratify her long cherished desire, and in the summer of the same year prepared to become a Carmelite. She spent the last weeks before entering the convent of the Order in Cologne once more with her family at Breslau. They were naturally in a state of intense anxiety, because the drive to eliminate the Jews from the national life was at its height. When Edith told her relatives of her intention to become a nun they took this to be her final break with her people. In fact it was exactly the opposite: she wanted to offer her life in Carmel as a sacrifice for the conversion of this same people which she loved intensely, and whose sufferings she shared with every fibre of her being. Ever since her conversion she had exercized an unspectacular but nevertheless powerful apostolate among her Jewish friends; this she would now continue even more intensely as a contemplative nun.

At her clothing, six months after she had entered, the Chapel of the Cologne Carmelites was filled by an illustrious congregation of intellectuals who had come to witness the total surrender to God of one of their own circle. Though she had been quite prepared to give up all her intellectual activities on entering Carmel, the Provincial of the Order now asked her to continue her philosophical work. She had brought with her a bulky manuscript entitled 'Potency and Act', in which she had examined these Thomist concepts and discussed their relationship to contemporary philosophy. In the next four years she completed this great work, which was finally published posthumously under the title *Finite and Eternal Being (Endliches und Ewiges Sein)*.

It is a heavy philosophical treatise of some five hundred pages, closely argued, in which she surveys the whole field of created and uncreated being in the attempt of a synthesis between St. Thomas and modern philosophy, mainly, of course, her own phenomenological school. After a cursory discussion of the concept of being in philosophical thought, she asks whether it is possible that the re-born philosophy of the Middle Ages and the new-born philosophy of the twentieth century could come together. She sees one of the main obstacles in the difference of terminology between scholasticism and modern philosophy, and takes great pains to give exact definitions of all the terms she uses. Going back to the original meanings of the Greek and Latin technical terms, she renders them into their German equivalents, a procedure illuminating to the German reader, but presenting great difficulties to the translator. She then discusses the being of which the ego is conscious, making the fullest use of the phenomenological method of meticulous analysis of which we give an example, taken from one of her earlier works, in the last part of this anthology. From transitory human being she leads the reader on to the eternal being of God, which may be known by the two ways of faith and of reasoning, the latter being the way of the Thomist proofs of the existence of God. The following section deals with the typically phenomenological concepts of essential and real being *(wesenhaftes und wirkliches Sein)*, and the later parts of the work are taken up with highly technical discussions of essence and substance, form and matter, the transcendentals, the meaning and foundation of individual being, and similar concepts. It is a work that can be understood and appreciated as well as criticized only by professional philosophers; but it is probably true to say that she herself would be the last person to claim that this synthesis between Thomism and modern philosophy was wholly successful. Nevertheless, it was a remarkable achievement, the more so if we consider the circumstances in which it was written. For the years between 1933 and 1938, when it was completed, were filled with deep personal anxiety, not so much for her own fate—though she had no illusions that Hitler would one day drag her even out of the enclosure of Carmel—but for the fate of her family and friends, who either emigrated or were living in constant fear of being arrested and put in a concentration camp. She often saw them in the parlour of her convent and listened to their sorrows. Yet, when she was once more sitting in her cell and continued writing her book her mind was serenely clear, moving in the philosopher's world of eternal truths, unaffected by the tragedies of the moment.

As the persecution of the Jews increased in violence, Edith Stein—or Sister Benedicta as she was now called—was not only herself in danger, but her presence in the convent also imperilled the whole Carmelite community. After the pogroms in November 1938 it was therefore decided that she should leave. On the last day of the year she was taken across the German frontier and received into the Carmelite convent in the Dutch town of Echt. She was well aware not only of her own precarious position, but also of the danger of the outside world, and decided to give all the help that she, an enclosed nun, could give to avert the disaster she foresaw. On Passion Sunday, scarcely three months after her flight from Cologne, she offered herself "to the Heart of Jesus as a sacrifice of expiation for true peace, that the reign of Antichrist may perish, if possible without a new World War, and a new order be established". The last years of her life were spent wholly in the spirit of this offering.

At Echt she was at first given little scope for intellectual activity; but in 1941, while Holland was firmly in the grip of the Nazis, she began to study mystical theology. The outcome of her work in this new field was an article on the Greek mystic theologian known as Dionysius the Areopagite, reproduced in this anthology, and a book on St. John of the Cross, called *The Science of the Cross (Kreuzeswissenschaft)*. This was written at the request of her superiors to commemorate the four hundredth anniversary, in 1942, of the birth of St. John of the Cross, the great mystic theologian of the Order. It is an interesting work, the work of a modern philosopher interpreting a mystic very largely by phenomenological methods. This unusual approach is responsible both for the advantages and the drawbacks of the book; for though it contributes freshness and originality to the presentation of its subject, it is also the cause of certain misunderstandings, especially on the relation between faith and contemplation and on the structure of the soul. Yet her phenomenological analyses, especially that of the night as a symbol of contemplation, prove that modern philosophical methods can throw light also on mystical states.

Sister Benedicta worked on *The Science of the Cross* until the very day when the Gestapo arrested her, on August 2nd, 1942. It was an act of reprisal for an outspoken pastoral of the Dutch bishops condemning the persecution of the Jews. At five o'clock in the evening, as the nuns were just going into choir to make their evening meditation, the Prioress was called to the parlour where two Gestapo officers demanded to see Sister Stein. At first the superior thought the visit had something to do with Sister Benedicta's proposed emigration to Switzerland, the preliminaries for which had been started some months before. She was soon disabused of this illusion; for the officers ordered Sister Benedicta to leave the convent immediately. She was given ten minutes to pack up the most necessary things and then taken to a concentration camp at Westerbork. Some prisoners who were fortunate enough to be released have preserved accounts of

their impression of Sister Benedicta. They stress her extraordinary
calm and the great charity with which she devoted herself to the
care of the children in the camp, whom she washed and dressed
as best she could, since their own mothers, beside themselves
with fear, were too distressed to do so. On August 7th she left
Westerbork in a train full of prisoners destined for Auschwitz;
there, according to the official records, she was gassed on August
9th in the same year.*

*   *   *   *   *

The present anthology has been compiled to give English-
speaking readers a representative picture of Edith Stein's intellectual and spiritual personality within a comparatively limited
space. This was no altogether easy task, for much of her work
is highly technical as well as diffuse. Edith Stein was, and
remained throughout her life, a phenomenologist, looking at
things with the eyes of the philosopher. She was a child of the
outgoing nineteenth century, a Jewish woman, yet an admirer
of Prussia, a feminist in her youth, given to abstract thought in
a way quite unusual in her sex, yet warmhearted and sensitive.
She grew up in the Germany of Wilhelm II, in the era preceding
the First World War that is almost more foreign to us than the
Middle Ages. Her studious character kept her away from many
of the ordinary amusements of young girls. She did not go to
dances, nor did she ever fall in love. Her feminine nature showed
herself in devotion to her venerated professor, Edmund Husserl,
but that was all. Her phenomenological training taught her to
look closely at the world and into herself, but in a detached
way, analyzing all she saw and pursuing impressions to their
roots. She herself once said her one desire was for truth; this she
sought in Husserl's philosophy and finally found in the Catholic
faith. Hence her religion, too, is cerebral; even her 'devotional'
writings, though penetrated by deep religious feeling, are the
writings of a thinker, well worked out, devoid of pious formulae.
Perhaps the most striking feature of her character as well as of

* For a full biography see the present editor's work *The Scholar and the Cross*,
Longmans 1955 ; American edition Newman Press, 1955.

her writings is her complete intellectual integrity, which attracted those who knew her in her lifetime, and which has come to attract thousands of readers after her death. She never makes a statement unless she is completely convinced of its truth; and this almost naive (in the good sense) sincerity leads her to criticize any view with which she cannot agree, however exalted the authority that holds it, whether it be the traditional Catholic teaching on evil as a negation, or St. Paul's statement that women are to be subject to men.

Many of her ideas were in advance of her time; and her great attempt to marry traditional Thomism and modern philosophy will probably point the way to further work in this direction. Her style is at its best and clearest in her spiritual and educational essays; we have tried as much as possible to smooth it for an English-speaking public; for her phenomenological habit of minute analysis does not make for easy reading. Since her two principal and at the same time most difficult works, *Finite and Eternal Being* and *The Science of the Cross,* will appear in an English translation in the U.S.A. in the future, we have included only very brief excerpts from these. There has been some hesitation about the arrangement of the anthology. We have finally decided not to follow the chronological order, since it seemed wiser to begin with the more easily accessible writings and lead from them to the more difficult ones. Hence we have started with her comparatively simple spiritual meditations, passed from there to her interpretation of mystical theology and to her educational essays, and lastly ascended into the rarefied atmosphere of purely phenomenological research.

*   *   *   *   *

The Mystery of Christmas and *The Prayer of the Church* were both written during her first years in the Carmel of Cologne, the essay on St. Elizabeth in 1931, before she became a lecturer at Muenster. They are among the finest specimens of twentieth century German religious writing, and at the same time faithfully reflect her own spiritual life and character. They have a firm intellectual and doctrinal basis, yet are practical, revealing a shrewd knowledge of human nature. *The Prayer of the Church* is remarkable for its blending of the Old Testament with the New Dispensation, of liturgical with 'individual' prayer, and the balance it maintains between the two. In this it is modern in the best sense of the term; for it is only in comparatively recent years that Catholics have begun to rediscover the spiritual treasures hidden in the Old Testament, that had been known so well to the Fathers of the Church. Through her Jewish upbringing Edith Stein was able to see in Christ not only the Son of God come to redeem the world, but also the Messias of her people whom the whole Old Testament foretells and to whom it points, so that the part played by 'the Law and the Prophets' in her personal spirituality as well as in her writings is exceptionally great and enriches her readers' outlook. These three pieces with which the Anthology opens attract by their thoughtful penetration of the Christian mysteries; they are without any devotional 'frills', yet imbued with deep religious feeling. The last of them, the essay on St. Elizabeth of Thuringia, is a gem of modern hagiography. It was written before the others, when Edith Stein was still a lecturer.

The article on Pseudo-Dionysius, *The Knowledge of God,* was written not quite two years before her death. Though it deals with mystical theology, this small treatise, too, is the work of a philosopher rather than of a theologian. It presents, in fact, a very interesting specimen of the phenomenological analysis of one of the most baffling and obscure writers. Unfortunately the German original of the article remained inaccessible to me; so the Editor of *The Thomist* (Washington, D.C.) graciously allowed me to use the translation by Rudolf Allers, published in his periodical in July 1946, with such alterations of style as were found necessary to bring it into line with the rest of the anthology. The symbolic theology of Pseudo-Dionysius is particulary suited to the phenomenological method, though theologians would not always agree with the author's views on the relations between faith and contemplation and similar subjects outside the province of phenomenology.

Her educational writings originated during her last years at

Speyer and her eighteen months at the Educational Academy at Muenster. In these latter the atmosphere changes: we are in the presence of a highly trained educationist who examines the root meaning of words, analyzes the ideas they represent, and frequently betrays feminist leanings. Nevertheless here, too, Edith Stein prefers to rest her argumentation on a Scriptural basis, and sometimes offers her own original exegesis. It is pointed out in the appropriate places where this deviates from the traditional Catholic doctrines.

In reading these essays it must be remembered that the climate of German Catholicism between the wars was very different from that of the English speaking countries and that even such to us preposterous sounding ideas as the priesthood for women were freely canvassed. Edith Stein was wide open to the trends of her time and discussed them with a freedom which may sometimes surprise those brought up in a more traditional atmosphere. It will cause all the more astonishment that in these educational essays she makes hardly any use of contemporary psychoanalysis. Both Freud and Jung were at the height of their influence in Germany at the time when Edith Stein wrote, yet their names are not so much as mentioned, and when she discusses 'types' she means by this something quite different from the Jungian concept.

This disregard of contemporary psychology is due to Edith Stein's mentality. She was a philosopher by temperament as well as by profession; hence her interest in psychological problems was that of a philosopher. She says herself in one of these essays: "The problems of philosophy begin where the work of the positive sciences leaves off". Hence her discussions may sometimes seem somewhat academic; yet in a time like our own so much more interested in psychological case history, it is perhaps very salutary to draw attention to the intellectual basis on which all psychological science rests. Besides, Edith Stein never remains completely theoretical, but after laying the theoretical foundations she has much practical advice to give especially on the education of girls, which generally culminates in her description of the Mother of God as the pattern of all true womanhood.

The final part of the anthology is devoted to Edith Stein's philosophical work. This will probably be found to be the most difficult for the reader unacquainted with modern German philosophy. The bulk of this section is made up by part of a treatise on the philosophical foundations of psychology she wrote in her late twenties, which shows unmistakably Husserl's phenomenological method in which she had been trained. It describes with meticulous accuracy the stream of consciousness as it presents itself to the observing mind of the phenomenological philosopher and the acts performed in the various mental processes, for example in responding to a stimulus, in taking cognizance of a fact, in reaching a decision and so forth. As has already been pointed out, this part presented many problems for the translator, as Edith Stein here succumbed to the habit of many German philosophers of coining their own language and replacing the internationally accepted terms of Latin or Greek origin by German neologisms which are practically untranslatable. That particular section of the earliest work of Edith Stein reproduced in this anthology has been chosen because it contains a passage on faith and its acceptance or refusal that seems to throw some light on her own psychological struggle before she finally decided to become a Catholic.

It is hoped that this selection of Edith Stein's writings will give the English speaking public an adequate idea of her thought and serve to make better known a great woman of our time whose life was spent in the service of truth and sealed by a heroic death as a victim of one of the totalitarian régimes of this century.

Hilda C. Graef.

Oxford,
December 1955.

SPIRITUAL WRITINGS

A. THE MYSTERY OF CHRISTMAS
Advent and Christmas

When the days are shortening, when, in a normal winter, the first snowflakes begin to fall, then men's thoughts, perhaps still shyly and hesitantly, will turn to Christmas. The very word diffuses a charm which few human hearts can resist. Even unbelievers, to whom the old story of the Child of Bethlehem means nothing, prepare for the feast, anxious to kindle a ray of joy here and there among their friends. Even weeks and months before, a warm current of love seems to traverse the whole earth. A feast of love and joy—this is the star to which all men look in the first months of winter. For the Christian, more especially for the Catholic, it means something else as well. The star will lead him to the manger with the Child that brings peace to the earth. Christian art presents it to us in innumerable pictures; ancient tunes, replete with all the charm of childhood, sing of it.

If we live with the Church, the Advent bells and hymns will stir a holy longing in our heart; and if we have been introduced to the inexhaustible source of the Liturgy, Isaias, the great prophet of the Incarnation, will rouse us day by day with his powerful warnings and promises: "Drop down dew, ye heavens, from above, and ye clouds, rain the just. The Lord is here, let us adore Him. Come, Lord, and do not delay. Rejoice, Jerusalem, with great joy, for thy Saviour comes to thee". From the seventeenth to the twenty-fourth of December the great O-antiphones of the Magnificat (O Wisdom, O Adonai, O root of Jesse, O key of David, O sunrise, O king of the nations) cry ever more longingly their "Come to deliver us". And it sounds with increasing promise: "Behold, everything is fulfilled" on the last Sunday of Advent, and finally: "Today you shall know that the Lord will come, and tomorrow you will see His glory". Yet, when on Christmas Eve the trees are lit and the presents exchanged, men are still longing for other lights, until the bells ring for the Midnight Mass, and the miracle of the Holy Night is renewed on the flower-decked altars with their burning candles: "And the Word was made flesh". This is the moment of bliss fulfilled.

Following the Incarnate Son of God

Perhaps every one of us has experienced such happiness at Christmas. But as yet heaven and earth are not united. The Star of Bethlehem is a star shining in a dark night, even today. On the second day the Church already lays aside her white festive vestments and clothes herself in the colour of blood, and on the fourth day in the purple of mourning. For the Crib of the Child is surrounded by martyrs. There is Stephen, the first martyr to follow his Lord to death; there are the innocent children, the babes of Bethlehem and Juda, who were cruelly slaughtered by the hands of brutal hangmen. What does this mean? Where is now the rejoicing of the heavenly hosts, the silent bliss of the Holy Night? Where is the peace on earth? Peace on earth to those of good will. But not all are of good will. For the Son of the eternal Father descended from the glory of heaven, because the mystery of iniquity had shrouded the earth in the darkness of night.

Darkness covered the earth, and He came as the Light that shines in the darkness, but the darkness did not comprehend Him. To those who received Him He brought light and peace; peace with the Father in Heaven, peace with all those who, like them, are children of light and children of the Father in Heaven, peace also in the intimate depths of the heart: but no peace with the children of darkness. To them the Prince of Peace does not bring peace but the sword. To them He is the stumbling block against which they knock and on which they are broken. This is the bitterly serious truth which ought not to be obscured by the poetic charm of the Child in the manger. The mystery of the Incarnation is closely linked to the mystery of iniquity. The night of sin appears all the more black and uncanny against the Light that is come down from heaven. The Child in the manger stretches out His small hands, and His smile seems to say even now the same as later the lips of the Man: "Come to me, all you that labour and are burdened". The poor shepherds have followed His call, when the radiance of the sky and the voice of the angel had announced the good tidings to them in the fields of Bethlehem, simply saying: "Let us go to Bethlehem" and setting out on their way. The kings from the far-away East followed the marvellous star with the same simple faith; on them all the hands of the Child poured the dew of His grace, and they "rejoiced with exceeding great joy". These hands give and demand at the same time: you wise men, lay down your wisdom and become simple like children; you kings, give your crowns and your treasures and bow down humbly before the King of kings; do not hesitate to take upon yourselves the sufferings and hardships His service entails. You children, who cannot yet give anything of your own free will, this Child's hands will take away your tender life even before it has really begun. It cannot be used better than to be sacrificed for the Lord of Life. These Child's hands say "Follow me" just as later the lips of the Man will say it. Thus He spoke to the "disciple whom the Lord loved", and who now belongs also to those around the Crib. St. John, the young man whose heart was as pure as a child's, followed without asking where and whither. He left his father's boat and followed the Lord on all His ways even to the summit of Golgotha. St. Stephen, too, heard these words "Follow me". He followed the Lord to do battle against the powers of darkness, the blindness of obstinate unbelief. He bore witness to Him with his words and with his blood; he followed Him also in His spirit of love which fights sin but loves the sinner, and intercedes for his murderer even in death.

Those kneeling around the crib are figures of light: the tender innocent children, the trustful shepherds, the humble kings, Stephen, the enthusiastic disciple, and John the apostle of love, all those who have followed the call of the Lord. They are opposed by the night of incomprehensible obstinacy and blindness: the scribes, who know indeed when and where the Saviour of the world is to be born, but who will not draw the conclusion: "Let us go to Bethlehem". King Herod, who would kill the Lord of Life. Ways part before the Child in the manger. He is the

King of kings, the Lord of life and death. He speaks His "Follow me!", and if a man is not for Him, he is against Him. He speaks also to us, and asks us to choose between light and darkness.

Union with God

We know not, and we should not ask before the time, where our earthly way will lead us. We know only this, that to those that love the Lord all things will work together to the good, and, further, that the ways by which the Saviour leads us point beyond this earth.

It is truly a marvellous exchange: the Creator of mankind, taking a body, gives us His Godhead. The Redeemer has come into the world to do this wonderful work. God became man, so that men might become children of God. One of us had broken the bond that made us God's children, one of us had to tie it again and pay the ransom. This could not be done by one who came from the old, wild and diseased trunk; a new branch, healthy and noble, had to be grafted into it. He became one of us, more than this, He became one with us. For this is the marvellous thing about the human race, that we are all one. If it were otherwise, if we were all autonomous individuals, living beside each other quite free and independent, the fall of the one could not have resulted in the fall of all. In that case, on the other hand, the ransom might have been paid for and imputed to us, but His justice could not have passed on to the sinners; no justification would have been possible. But He came to be *one* mysterious Body with us: He our Head, we His members. If we place our hands into the hands of the divine Child, if we say our Yes to His Follow Me, then we are His, and the way is free for His divine Life to flow into us.

This is the beginning of eternal life in us. It is not yet the beatific vision in the light of glory; it is still the darkness of faith; but it is no longer of this world, it means living in the kingdom of God. This kingdom began on earth when the blessed Virgin spoke her "Be it unto me", and she was its first handmaid. And all those who have confessed the Child by word and deed before and after His birth, St. Joseph, St. Elizabeth with her son and all those surrounding the crib, have entered the kingdom of God. The reign of the divine King showed itself to be different from what people had expected it to be when they read the Psalms and the Prophets. The Romans remained masters in the land, high priests and scribes continued to oppress the poor. Those who belonged to the Lord bore their kingdom of heaven invisibly within them. Their earthly burden was not taken away from them; on the contrary, many another was added to it; but within them there was a winged power that made the yoke sweet and the burden light. The same happens today with every child of God. The divine life that is kindled in the soul is the light that has come into the darkness, the miracle of the Holy Night. If we have it in us, we understand what is meant when men speak about it. For the others everything that can be said of it is an incomprehensible stammering. The whole Gospel of St. John is such a stammering about the eternal light that is love and life. God in us and we in Him, this is our share in God's kingdom, which is founded on the Incarnation.

Union in God

Union with God: this is the first fruit. But a second results immediately from this. If Christ is the Head and we are the members of the Mystical Body, then we are related to each other as such; we human beings are one with each other in God, sharing one divine life. If God is in us, and if He is love, then it cannot be otherwise than that we love the brethren. Therefore our love of men is the measure of our love of God. But it is different from the natural love of men. The natural love is given to this or that person who is united to us by a blood relationship, or is near to us because our characters are akin or we have common interests. The others are 'strangers' who do not concern us, whose character we may even loathe, so that we keep them as much as possible at a distance. For the Christian there is no stranger. Whoever is near us and needing us most is our 'neighbour'; it does not matter whether he is related to us or not, whether we like him or not, whether he is morally worthy of our help or not. The love of Christ knows no limits. It never ends, it does not shrink from ugliness and filth. He came for sinners, not for the just. And if the love of Christ is in us, we shall do as He did and seek the lost sheep.

Natural love strives to have the loved one to itself and to possess him as undividedly as possible. Christ came to win back lost mankind for the Father; if we love with His love, we shall want men for God and not for ourselves. This is, indeed, also the surest way to possess them for ever; for if we have found shelter for a person in God, we shall be one with him in God; whereas the desire to conquer will often, in the long run always, result in loss. It is the same with another's soul as with one's own and with every external good: if we are anxious to gain and keep it we shall lose it. If we give it to God, we shall gain it.

Thy Will Be Done

With this we come upon a third sign of being a child of God. The first was union with God; the second was that all are one in God. Now the third: "By this I know that you love me, if you keep my commandments". If we are children of God we shall be led by His hand, doing His will, not our own. We shall place every care and hope in Him and be no longer troubled about ourselves and our future. This is the reason why God's children are free and happy. But how few even of the truly pious, even of those ready for heroic sacrifices, possess this freedom. They all walk as if they were bent down by the heavy burden of their cares and duties. They all know the parable of the birds of the air and the lilies of the field. But if they meet someone without capital or pension or insurance, and who yet lives without worrying about the future, they shake their heads as if that were something extraordinary. Indeed, if we expect from the Father in heaven that He will always provide for the income and station in life which we ourselves consider desirable, we may be very much mistaken. Only then can our trust in God remain unshaken, if it includes being prepared to accept absolutely everything

from the hand of the Father. For He alone knows what is good
for us. And if one day want and the lack of even the necessaries
of life should be better for us than a comfortably secure income,
or if we should need failure and humiliation rather than honour
and reputation, we must be prepared also for this. If we do this,
we can live for the present without being burdened by the future.

The words "Thy will be done" must be the rule of the Christian's life in all their fullness. They must be the principle that
regulates his day from morning to night, the course of the year
and his whole life. It then becomes the Christian's only concern.
For all other cares the Lord will make Himself responsible; this
alone will remain with us as long as we live. From the objective
point of view it is not absolutely certain that we shall always
remain in the ways of God. Just as the first man and woman
became estranged from God though they had been His children,
so every one of us is always balancing, as it were, on the edge of
the knife between nothingness and the fullness of the divine life.
Sooner or later we shall be feeling this also subjectively. In the
infancy of the spiritual life, when we have just begun to surrender ourselves to the guidance of God, we feel His guiding hand
very strongly; it is clear as daylight what we have to do and what
to avoid. But it will not remain like this. If we belong to Christ,
we have to live the whole Christ-life. We must mature into His
Manhood, we must one day begin the Way of the Cross to
Gethsemani and to Golgotha. And all sufferings that come from
without are as nothing compared with the dark night of the
soul, when the divine light no longer shines, and the voice of the
Lord no longer speaks. God is there, but He is hidden and silent.
Why is this so? We are speaking of the mysteries of God, and
these cannot be completely penetrated. But we may well look a
little into them. God became Man in order once more to give us
a share in His life. This is the beginning, and this is the last end.

But between these there is something else. Christ is God and
Man, and if we would share His life, we must share both in the
divine and the human life. The human nature which He took
enabled Him to suffer and to die. The divine nature which He
possessed from eternity gave His suffering and death infinite

27

value and redemptive power. Christ's suffering and death are continued in His mystical Body and in each of His members. Every man must suffer and die. But if he is a *living* member of the Body of Christ, his suffering and death will receive redemptive power from the divinity of the Head. This is the objective reason why all the saints have desired to suffer. This is not a pathological pleasure in suffering. It is true, to natural reason it appears as a perversion. But in the light of the mystery of salvation it shows itself to be highly reasonable. And thus the man who is united to Christ will remain unmoved even in the dark night of feeling estranged from, and abandoned by God. Perhaps divine providence is using his agony to deliver another, who is truly a prisoner cut off from God. Therefore we will say: "Thy will be done" even, and particularly so, in the darkest night.

Means of Salvation

But can we still say "Thy will be done" even when we no longer have any certainty what God's will asks of us? Do we still have the means of keeping in His ways when the inner light is extinguished? There are such means; and they are so effective that, though the possibility of going astray remains in principle, it yet becomes infinitely improbable in fact. For God has come to redeem us, to unite us to Himself and to each other, to conform our will to His. He knows our nature. He reckons with it, and has therefore given us every help necessary to reach our goal.

The divine Child has become a *teacher* and has told us what to do. In order to penetrate a whole human life with the divine life it is not enough to kneel once a year before the crib and let ourselves be captivated by the charm of the holy night. To achieve this, we must be in daily contact with God, listening to the words He has spoken and which have been transmitted to us, and obeying them. We must, above all, pray as the Saviour Himself has taught us so insistently. "Ask and it shall be given you". This is the certain promise of being heard. And if we pray every day with all our heart: "Lord, thy will be done" we may well trust that we shall not fail to do God's will even when we no longer have subjective certainty.

More: Christ has not left us orphans. He has sent His Spirit, who teaches us all truth. He has founded His Church which is guided by His Spirit, and has ordained in it His representatives by whose mouth His Spirit speaks to us in human words. In His Church He has united the faithful into one community and wants them to support each other. Thus we are not alone, and if the confidence in our own understanding and even in our own prayer fails us, the power of obedience and intercession will assist us.

"And the word was made flesh". This became reality in the stable of Bethlehem. But it has also been fulfilled in another form. "He who eats my flesh and drinks my blood has eternal life". The Saviour, knowing that we are and remain men who have daily to struggle with our weaknesses, aids our humanity in a manner truly divine. Just as our earthly body needs its daily bread, so the divine life in us must be constantly fed. "This is the living bread that came down from heaven". If we make It truly our daily bread, the mystery of Christmas, the Incarnation of the Word, will daily be re-enacted in us. And this, it seems, is the surest way to remain in constant union with God, and to grow every day more securely and more deeply into the mystical Body of Christ. I am well aware that many will think this an exaggerated demand. In practice it means for most of those who start this habit that they will have to rearrange their outer and inner life completely. But this is just what it is meant to do. Is it really demanding too much to make room in our life for the Eucharistic Saviour, so that He may transform our life into His own? We have time for so many useless things: we read senseless rubbish in books, periodicals and newspapers, sit in cafés and chat for a quarter or half an hour in the street. All these are distractions by which one wastes time and strength. Should it really be impossible to save an hour in the morning in which one is not distracted but recollected, in which one does not spend oneself but gathers strength sufficient to carry one through the whole day?

It is true, more is needed for this than just the one hour. We must live from one such hour to the next in such a way that we shall be allowed to come again. It is no longer possible to 'let ourselves go', even only for a little while. We cannot escape the judgement of a person with whom we are in daily contact. Even without words we feel what others think of us. We shall try to adapt ourselves to our surroundings, and if this proves impossible it will be torture to live together. Thus it is also in the daily intercourse with our Lord. We shall become ever more sensitive to what pleases and displeases Him. If before we had been, on the whole, quite satisfied with ourselves, this will now become very different. We shall find much that is bad and change it if possible. And we shall discover many things that we cannot think are satisfactory, and which are yet so hard to change. And so we shall gradually become very small and humble, as well as patient and indulgent with the motes in the eyes of others, because we are busy with the beam in our own. And finally we shall learn even to bear with ourselves in the light of the divine presence, and to give ourselves up to the divine mercy which can deal with all the difficulties that are too much for our own strength. It is a long way from the smug self-satisfaction of the 'good Catholic' who 'does his duties', reads a 'good paper', etc., but apart from that does what he likes, to a life guided and provided by the hand of God, in the simplicity of the child and the humility of the publican. But whoever has walked in this way will no more turn back.

Thus, being a child of God means to become small and at the same time to become great. Living eucharistically means quite naturally to leave the narrowness of one's own life and to grow into the breadth of the Christ life. If we seek the Lord in His house, we shall not always occupy Him only with ourselves and our own affairs. We shall begin to be interested in His affairs. If we take part in the daily sacrifice, we shall be drawn quite without effort into the liturgical life. Within the cycle of the Church's Year the prayers and rites of the services present to us the story of our salvation again and again and cause us to penetrate ever more deeply into their meaning. The sacrifice of the Mass impresses on us time and again the central mystery of our faith, the pivot of the world's history, the mystery of the Incarnation and Redemption. Who could assist at the Holy sacrifice with a receptive mind and heart and not himself be filled with the sacrificial spirit, burning with the desire that his own small personal life should be merged into the great work of the Saviour?

The Christian mysteries are an indivisible whole. If we become immersed in one, we are led to all the others. Thus the way from Bethlehem leads inevitably to Golgotha, from the crib to the Cross. When the blessed Virgin brought the Child to the temple, Symeon prophesied that her soul would be pierced by a sword, that this Child was set for the fall and the resurrection of many, for a sign that would be contradicted. His prophecy announced the Passion, the fight between light and darkness that already showed itself before the crib.

In some years Candlemas and Septuagesima are celebrated almost together, the feast of the Incarnation and the preparation of the Passion. The star of Bethlehem shines in the night of sin. The shadow of the Cross falls on the light that shines from the crib. The light is extinguished in the darkness of Good Friday, but it rises all the more brilliantly as the sun of grace on the morning of the Resurrection. The way of the incarnate Son of God leads through the Cross and Passion to the glory of the Resurrection. In His company the way of every one of us, indeed of all mankind, leads through suffering and death to this same glorious goal.

B. THE PRAYER OF THE CHURCH

By him, and with him, and in him,
is to thee, God, the Father almighty,
in the unity of the Holy Ghost,
all honour and glory.

With these solemn words the priest concludes the prayers of the Mass that centre in the mysterious event of transubstantiation. At the same time they summarize in the briefest form the essence of the Church's prayer, which is the honour and glory offered to the triune God through, with and in Christ. Even though these words are addressed to the Father, we cannot glorify Him without at the same time glorifying also the Son and the Holy Ghost. For the glory that is praised here the Father communicates to the Son, and both to the Holy Ghost throughout eternity.

All praise that is given to God is offered by, with and in Christ. God is praised *by* Him, because mankind has access to the Father only through Christ, and because His divine-human being and redemptive work is the most perfect glorification of the Father. He is praised *with* Him, because every genuine prayer is a fruit of union with Christ which it also makes more intimate; secondly, because all praise of the Son is at the same time praise of the Father and *vice versa*. He is praised *in* Him, because the praying Church is Christ Himself, every praying individual being a member of His mystical Body, and because the Father is in the Son, who is the effulgence of the Father who makes His glory visible. The twofold meaning of the 'by', 'with' and 'in' is the clear expression of the mediatorship of the Godman.

The prayer of the Church is the prayer of Christ living in her. Its prototype is the prayer of Christ during His human life.

1. The Prayer of the Church as Liturgy and Eucharist

We know from the Gospel accounts that Christ prayed as a

believing Jew and faithful follower of the Law used to pray. For Judaism had and still has its richly developed liturgy for public as well as domestic worship, for the great feasts as well as for every day. Ever since He had been a child He had gone to Jerusalem with His parents to celebrate the great feasts in the Temple, and later He did the same with His disciples. With holy joy He must surely have chanted with His companions the jubilant hymn in which the pilgrims anticipated their happiness: "I rejoiced when it was said to me: We will go into the house of the Lord". (Ps. 121: 1). His last meeting with His disciples was devoted to the fulfilment of the most sacred religious duties, the solemn paschal meal by which the deliverance from the bondage of Egypt was commemorated. The New Testament account of it shows that He recited the ancient prayers of blessing which are still said today over bread, wine, and the fruits of the field: "Praised be Thou, Eternal One, our God, King of the world, who bringest forth bread out of the earth", ". . . who didst create the fruit of the vine". And perhaps just this meeting will give us the deepest insight into the prayer of Christ, and so the key to the understanding of the prayer of the Church.

"And while they were at supper, Jesus took bread and blessed and broke and gave to his disciples and said: Take ye and eat. This is my body. And taking the chalice, he gave thanks and gave to them, saying: Drink ye all of this. For this is my blood of the new testament, which shall be shed for many unto remission of sins". (Matth. 26: 26-28).

The blessing and distribution of bread and wine was part of the rite of the paschal meal. But both receive here a completely new meaning. With this begins the life of the Church. It is true, as a spirit-filled visible community she will appear only at Pentecost. But here, during the paschal meal, the branches are grafted into the vine, and only this act will make possible the outpouring of the Spirit. On the lips of Christ the old prayers of blessing have become words that infuse life. The fruits of the earth have become His Flesh and Blood, they are filled with His life. The visible creation, which He entered through the Incarnation, is now united to Him in a new, mysterious way. The materials that serve to build up the human body have become radically transformed, and through their faithful reception men, too, are changed: they are brought into unity of life with Christ, they are themselves filled with His divine life. The life-creating power of the Word is linked to the sacrifice. The Word has become flesh in order to surrender the life He took, in order to give Himself and the creation that has been reconciled through His sacrifice, as a sacrifice of praise to the Creator. Through the Last Supper of the Lord the paschal meal of the Old Covenant has been transformed into the paschal meal of the New Dispensation, into the sacrifice of the Cross on Golgotha, into those joyful meals of the time between Easter and the Ascension, when the disciples recognized the Lord in the breaking of the bread, and into the sacrifice of the Mass and Holy Communion.

When the Lord took the cup, He gave thanks. We may think of the words of blessing which contain a thanks to the Creator. We know, too, however, that Christ would give thanks when He lifted up His eyes to the Father in heaven before performing a miracle; for example before the raising of Lazarus (John 11: 41f.). He gives thanks, because He knows beforehand that His prayer is answered. He gives thanks for the divine power He bears within Him, and by which He will show forth before men the omnipotence of the Creator. He thanks *for* the work of Redemption which He is allowed to work, and *through* this work, which itself glorifies the triune Godhead, because it renews His deformed image in perfect beauty. Thus the whole permanent sacrificial surrender of Christ, on the Cross, in the Mass and in the eternal glory of heaven, may be seen as one sole great thanksgiving, as a Eucharist: a thanksgiving for creation, redemption and perfection. He offers Himself on behalf of the whole created world whose prototype He is, and into which He descended in order to renew it from within and lead it to perfection. But He also calls this whole created world to pay the homage of gratitude due to the Creator in union with Him. Even the Old Covenant was aware of this eucharistic character of prayer. The marvellous edifice of the Tabernacle and later of the Solomonic

Temple, built according to divine instructions, was regarded as an image of the whole creation, surrounding its Lord in service and worship. The tent around which the people of Israel used to camp during their wanderings in the desert was called "the tabernacle of the testimony" (Exodus 38: 21). It was the "lower dwelling" as opposed to the "upper dwelling". The Psalmist sings: "I have loved, O Lord, the beauty of thy house: and the place where thy glory dwelleth" (Ps. 25: 8), because the Tabernacle is equated with the creation of the world. Just as, according to the creation narrative, heaven was spread out like a carpet, so carpets were prescribed for the walls of the Tabernacle. As the waters of the earth were separated from the waters of heaven, so the curtain separated the Holy of Holies from the outer rooms. The "sea of brass" imitated the sea hemmed in by its coasts. The seven-armed candle-stick in the tent stands for the lights of heaven; lambs and birds represent the crowds of living creatures in the water, on the earth and in the air. And as the earth was assigned to man, so the high priest stands in the sanctuary, anointed to work and serve before God. Moses blessed, anointed and sanctified the finished dwelling, as the Lord had blessed and sanctified the work of His hands on the seventh day. This dwelling was to be God's witness on earth, even as heaven and earth are His witnesses (cf. Deuteronomy 30: 19).

In the place of Solomon's Temple, Christ has built a temple of living stones, the communion of Saints. He stands in its centre as the eternal High Priest, He Himself is the eternal sacrifice on its altar. And again the whole creation is included in the solemn service of the liturgy. The fruits of the earth that are the mysterious offering, the flowers and the candlesticks with their candles, the carpets and the curtain, the consecrated priest and the anointing and blessing of the house of God. Even the cherubim are there. Formed by the hand of the artist, their visible shapes keep watch by the Blessed Sacrament. As their living images the 'angelic monks' surround the altar of sacrifice, so that the divine praises shall no less cease on earth than they do in heaven. The solemn prayers they offer as the mouthpiece of the Church surround the holy sacrifice, penetrating and sancti-

35

fying also all other 'daily work', so that prayer and work form one single *opus Dei*, one single 'liturgy'. Their readings from the Holy Scriptures and the Fathers, from the ecclesiastical records and the doctrinal statements of the Popes are a great, ever increasing song of praise in honour of divine providence and the progressive realization of the plan of salvation. Their morning hymns again call the whole creation to unite in the praise of the Lord: the mountains and hills, the rivers and streams, sea and land and all their inhabitants, clouds and winds, rain and snow, all the nations of the earth, all estates and races of men, finally even the inhabitants of heaven, the angels and saints: They all are to take their share, not through their man-made images or human representatives, but in their own persons in the great Eucharist of Creation; or rather, we are to join through our liturgy in their eternal praise of God. We—this means not only the religious, who are specially called to this solemn praise of God, but all Christian people. When, on the great feasts, they fill the cathedral and abbey churches, when they gladly take their active share in the new, popular liturgical functions, they show that they are conscious of their vocation to praise God. The liturgical unity of the heavenly and the earthly Church which both give thanks to God 'through Christ' find its clearest expression in the Preface and the Sanctus of the Mass.

Nevertheless, the liturgy leaves no doubt about it that we are not yet perfect citizens of the heavenly Jerusalem, but pilgrims on our way to our eternal home. We always need a preparation before we may dare to lift up our eyes to the luminous heights and to join the heavenly choirs in their Holy, Holy, Holy. All created things that are used in the divine service must be set apart from profane usage by being blessed and sanctified. Before ascending the altar steps the priest must purify himself by the confession of sins, in which he is joined by the faithful; before each new stage in the course of the sacrificial action he must repeat the prayer for forgiveness of sins for himself, for those around him, and for all who are to share in the fruits of sacrifice. The sacrifice itself is a sacrifice of atonement, which transforms the faithful together with the gifts, opening heaven for them and

36

preparing them to make a thanksgiving that is pleasing to God. All that we need in order to be received into the community of the blessed spirits is summarized in the seven petitions of Our Father, which the Lord did not recite in His own name, but for our instruction. We say it before Holy Communion, and if we say it sincerely and from our heart, receiving Holy Communion in the right spirit, it will bring us the fulfilment of all the petitions: it will deliver us from evil, because it cleanses us from guilt and gives the peace of the heart which takes the sting out of all other evils; it brings us the forgiveness of the sins we have committed (it is of course presupposed that we are not burdened with grievous sin; else we could not receive Holy Communion in the right spirit) and strengthens us against temptations; it is itself the Bread of Life which we need every day in order to grow into the eternal life; it makes our will a pliable instrument of the divine will, and thus establishes God's kingdom in us, giving us pure lips and a pure heart to glorify His holy name.

Thus it again becomes evident that sacrificial action, the sacrificial meal and the divine praises are intimately united. For by participating in the sacrifice and in the sacrificial meal every soul becomes a living stone of God's city and itself a temple of God.

2. *The Solitary Converse with God as Prayer of the Church*

The fact that the individual human soul is a temple of God opens up an entirely new and glorious view. The prayer life of Jesus was to be our key to the understanding of the prayer of the Church. We have seen that Christ took part in the appointed public worship of His people (i.e. in what is commonly called the liturgy); by bringing this into the closest union with His own sacrificial surrender He gave it its real and perfect meaning, that is creation's homage of gratitude to its Creator, and thus transformed the Liturgy of the Old into that of the New Covenant.

Yet Jesus did not only take part in the official public worship. Perhaps even more frequently the Gospels record His solitary prayer in the stillness of the night, in the freedom of high mountains, in the desert, far away from men. The public activity of

Jesus was preceded by forty days and nights of prayer (Matth. 4:1ff.). Before choosing and sending out His twelve Apostles, He retired to pray in the solitude of the mountains (Luke 6:12). He prepared Himself for the way to Golgotha by His hour of prayer on the Mount of Olives. What He said to His Father in the hardest hour of His life has been revealed to us in a few short words that have been given us as a guiding light for our own dark hours: "Father, if thou wilt, remove this chalice from me: but yet not my will but thine be done". (Luke 22:42). Like a flash of lightning they illuminate for a moment the innermost life of our Lord's soul, the unfathomable mystery of His divine-human being and His dialogue with the Father. Surely this dialogue had lasted uninterruptedly throughout His life. Christ was praying interiorly not only when He had left the crowds, but also when He was moving among them. And once He has allowed us a long, profound insight into this secret conversation.

It was not long before the hour on the Mount of Olives, indeed immediately before going there, after the Last Supper which, as we have just seen, was the real hour of the Church's birth. "Having loved his own . . . he loved them unto the end". (John 13:1). He knew it was their last time together, and He wanted to give them as much as He possibly could. He had to constrain Himself not to say even more. But He knew that they could not bear more, indeed that they were unable to comprehend even the little He did say. The Spirit of Truth had to come to open their eyes to this. And after He had said and done to them all He could, He raised His eyes to heaven and spoke to the Father in their presence. (John 17). We call these words the highpriestly prayer of Jesus. For this solitary converse with God, too, has its type in the Old Covenant. Once a year, on the greatest and most solemn feast, the Day of Atonement, the high priest entered the holy of holies, standing before the face of the Lord, "to pray for himself and his house, and for the whole congregation of Israel" (Lev. 16:17), to sprinkle the mercy seat with the blood of the young bull and the buck-goat which he had to slaughter before, and thus to "expiate the sanctuary" from his own sins and those of his house, and "from the uncleanness of the children of Israel, and from their transgressions, and all their sins". (Lev. 16: 16). No man was to be in the tabernacle (that is in the holy, which was before the holy of holies) when the high priest went into the presence of God in this most awesome and exalted place, which no one except himself was allowed to enter, and even he only in this one hour. And even then he had to offer incense, "that . . . the cloud and vapour thereof may cover the oracle . . . and he may not die" (ibid. 16: 13). This solitary conversation took place in the deepest secrecy.

The Day of Atonement is the Old Testament type of Good Friday. The bull that was slaughtered for the sins of the people represented the immaculate Lamb of God, also probably that other one, appointed by lot and driven into the desert laden with the sins of the people.* The high priest from the house of Aaron is the shadow of the eternal High Priest. As, at the last supper, Christ anticipated His sacrificial death, so He anticipated also the highpriestly prayer. Being Himself without sin, He did not need to offer a sin offering for Himself; He did not need to wait for the hour appointed by the Law and to enter the holy of holies of the temple. He stands always and everywhere before the face of God, His own soul is the holy of holies; it is not only God's dwelling, but essentially and indissolubly united to Him. He needs no protective cloud of smoke to hide Him before the Lord: He sees the unveiled face of the Eternal One without having anything to fear; the sight of the Father will not kill Him. And He opens the seal of the high priesthood: all His own may hear what He says to the Father in the holy of holies of His heart; they are to realize what is the issue and to learn how to speak to the Father in their own hearts. The highpriestly prayer of the Saviour reveals the mystery of the interior life: the circumincession of the divine Persons and the indwelling of God in the soul. In these hidden depths the work of salvation was prepared and accomplished in secrecy and silence; and so it will be continued until, at the end of time, all will have been truly consummated into being one. In the eternal silence of the interior

* The reference is to the goat of Lev. 16: 10.   Ed.

divine life the plan of Redemption was decided. In the hiddenness of the quiet chamber of Nazareth the power of the Holy Ghost came upon the Virgin praying in solitude, and brought about the Incarnation of the Saviour. Assembled round the silently praying Virgin, the nascent Church awaited the promised coming of the Holy Ghost that was to vivify them unto inner enlightenment and fruitful external activity. In the night of blindness that God had laid on his eyes, Saul awaited in solitary prayer the answer of the Lord to his question: "What wilt thou have me to do?" In solitary prayer Peter was prepared for his mission to the Gentiles. And so it remains throughout the centuries. In the solitary conversation of consecrated souls there are prepared those widely visible events of the Church's history that renew the face of the earth. The Virgin who kept every God-sent word in her heart is the pattern of those listening souls in whom the highpriestly prayer of Jesus is for ever renewed. And women who, like her, forget themselves completely in their contemplation of the life and passion of Christ, the Lord has chosen with preference to be His instruments for doing great things in the Church, such as St. Bridget and St. Catherine of Siena. And when St. Teresa, the powerful reformer of her Order in the time of the great apostasy, desired to come to the aid of the Church, she saw the means to that in the renewal of the true interior life. The news of the ever increasing apostasy grieved her: "And as though I could do anything, or were something, I asked the Lord with many tears and entreated Him to remedy this great evil. It seemed to me that I would have risked a thousand lives to save a single one of all the souls that were being lost there. And, seeing that I was a woman and incapable of doing anything, and as my whole longing was that at least a few souls should be very good, I decided to do what was possible, namely to follow the evangelical counsels with the greatest possible perfection, and to strive that the few nuns who are here together, should do the same . . . I trusted in the infinite mercy of God, and, constantly praying for those who protect the Church as well as for the preachers and learned men who defend her, we will all aid our Lord as well as we can, whereas His persecutors crucify Him anew, as it were. Oh my dearest Sisters, help me to entreat our Lord; for to this purpose He has gathered you here, this is your vocation".*

It seemed necessary to her "that here should be done the same as in time of war, when enemies have invaded the whole country. For then the prince of the land withdraws . . . into a city which he causes to be strongly fortified. From there he sometimes makes a sally on the enemies; and as those in the city are all picked men, they alone do more than when they were among many cowardly soldiers, and thus is often gained a victory . . . Now why have I said this? That you, my Sisters, may see from this what we should ask from God: namely that of the still good Christians who are in the fortress none should go over to the enemy; further, that the Lord may cause the captains of this fortress . . . that is the preachers and theologians, greatly to advance in His ways, and, since most of them are religious, He may give them His grace to make great progress in the perfection to which they are called . . . They must live among men and associate with them . . . and sometimes they have even to adapt themselves to people in external matters. And do you think, my daughters, it is easy to live and move in the world, to busy oneself with worldly concerns . . . and yet interiorly to remain foreign to the world . . . to be not like a man but like an angel? For if they were not thus, they did not deserve the name of 'captains', and then God forbid that they should come forth from their cells, because they would do more harm than good. Nowadays one ought not to perceive any imperfections in those who have to act as teachers . . . For with whom have they to do but with the world? The world, of this they may be convinced, will overlook no imperfection in them and will not forgive them anything. Many of their good qualities will be overlooked, perhaps they will not even be accounted as good; but we cannot hope that men will not notice any fault or imperfection. I am surprised to see how well instructed people in the world are nowadays in perfection, not to practise it . . . but to blame

* *The Way of Perfection*, ch. 1. I have translated from the German, as the text differs slightly from the English translation of Allison Peers. Ed.

41

others . . . Hence you may not believe that in the hard fight which those now enter only a little divine help were needed; on the contrary, they need much of it. . . . Hence I ask you for the love of the Lord, implore His Majesty that He may hear our prayer. Though I am miserable, I yet ask the Lord for this, for here His honour and the good of His Church are at stake, which are my only desires . . . Unless your prayers, your longings, your scourgings and fasts have not the aim of which I have spoken, you need not think that you fulfil the purpose for which the Lord has assembled you here".*

What was it that inspired this nun, who had been living in prayer in her cloistered cell for so many years, with the ardent desire to do something for the cause of the Church? What made her realize the needs and demands of her time with such penetration? Precisely the fact that she was living a life of prayer, that she let herself be drawn ever more deeply into the inner parts of her 'Interior Castle', even unto that hidden chamber where He could say to her: "that it was time she took upon her His affairs as if they were her own, and that He would take her affairs upon Himself". The person who gives herself to the Lord without reserve, He chooses to be His instrument for building His Kingdom. He alone knows how much the prayer of St. Teresa and her daughters has contributed to preserve Spain from the so-called Reformation, and how great has been its power in the violent wars of religion in France, in the Netherlands and in Germany. The official historians are silent about these invisible and unaccountable powers. But they are known to the trust of the faithful and the patiently examining and carefully weighing judgement of the Church. And our own time, seeing that all else fails, finds itself more and more urged to hope for ultimate salvation from these hidden sources.

3. Inner Life and External Form and Action

The work of Redemption is accomplished in a hidden way and

---

* ibid., ch. 3 The two passages I have cited are read in our Order on Ember Days.

in silence. The living stones from which grows the Kingdom of God, the chosen instruments that further the building, are prepared in the silent converse of the heart with God. The mystical stream, which flows through all the centuries, is no spurious side-current that has strayed from the prayer life of the Church—it is her very life-blood. If it breaks through the traditional forms, it does so because the spirit that blows where it listeth is living in it: He who has fashioned all the traditional forms must ever fashion new ones. Without Him there would be neither Liturgy nor Church. Was not the soul of the royal psalmist a harp whose strings sounded as they were touched by the gentle breath of the Holy Ghost? From the over-flowing heart of the Virgin full of grace comes forth the exultant hymn of the *Magnificat*. The prophetical song *Benedictus* opened the dumb lips of the old priest when the angel's secret word became visible reality. Whatever ascended from the spirit-filled heart and expressed itself in word and song is transmitted from mouth to mouth. It is the Divine Office to see to it that it should continue to sound from generation to generation. Thus is formed the mystical stream of the polyphonous, ever-increasing song of praise to the triune God, the Creator, Redeemer and Perfecter. Therefore it is inadmissible to oppose, as 'subjective' piety, the interior prayer that is free from traditional forms to the liturgy as the 'objective prayer' of the Church. Every genuine prayer is prayer of the Church; through every genuine prayer something happens in the Church, and it is the Church herself who prays in it, for it is the Holy Ghost living in her, who in every individual soul "asketh for us with unspeakable groanings". Precisely this is authentic prayer, for "no man can say The Lord Jesus, but by the Holy Ghost". What is the prayer of the Church, if not the self-giving of the great lovers to the God who is Love?

The limitless loving surrender to God and the divine reward, the perfect and constant union, this is the highest elevation of the heart accessible to us, the highest stage of prayer. The souls that have achieved this are truly the heart of the Church; they are filled with the highpriestly love of Christ. Being hidden with Christ in God, they cannot do otherwise than radiate into the hearts of others the divine love with which they are filled, and so co-operate unto perfecting all into unity in God, which was and is the great concern of Jesus Christ. Thus Marie Antoinette de Geuser had understood her vocation. She had to perform this highest task of the Christian in the midst of the world; and her way is certainly an encouraging example to all who today feel impelled to aid the Church by the radical practice of their interior life, and to whom it is not given to follow this call in the security of the cloister. The soul which, in the highest stage of mystic prayer, has entered into the "peaceful activity of the divine life" thinks of nothing else but to give itself to the apostolate to which God has called it.

"This is the tranquillity of order, and at the same time activity that is freed from all fetters. The soul fights in peace, because it works entirely in harmony with the eternal providence. It knows that the will of God works itself out wholly to His greater glory, for even though the human will, as it were erects barriers for the divine omnipotence, yet omnipotence conquers and creates a magnificent work from the material that is left to It. This victory of the divine power over human freedom, which He yet permits to act, is one of the most marvellous and adorable traits of the divine plan for the world".* When Marie Antoinette de Geuser wrote this letter, she was nearing the threshold of eternity; only a thin veil separated her from that last perfection which we call the life of glory.

In the blessed spirits that have entered into the unity of the divine inner life, all is one: rest and activity, vision and work, silence and speech, listening and self-communication, the surrender of love that receives and the love that gives itself in the praise of gratitude. As long as we are still on the way, we are subject to the bondage of time, and the farther we are from the goal the more so. The fullness of the divine life can be realized in us only successively, the many members have to complement each other. We need the hours when we listen in silence and let the divine work take effect in us until it craves to bear fruit in the sacrifice of praise and action. We need the traditional

* Marie de la Trinité, *Lettres de ' Consummata ' à une Carmélite 1930.*

forms, we must participate in the set forms of public worship so that the inner life may be kindled in us, that it may remain in the right order and find adequate expression. The solemn divine praise must have its homes on earth, where it is developed to the highest perfection of which men are capable. From there it can rise to heaven on behalf of the whole Church and have its effect on her members, kindling the interior life and inviting external participation. But it must be quickened from within also in these places, where opportunity should be given for silent penetration. Else it would degenerate into lifeless, formal lip service. The homes of the interior life give protection against this danger; they are the places where souls live before God in solitude and silence, in order to be the all-enlivening love in the heart of the Church.

Now Christ is the way to the interior life and to the choirs of blessed spirits who sing the eternal *Sanctus*. His Blood is the curtain by which we enter the holy of holies of the divine life. In baptism and in the sacrament of penance It cleanses us from sin, opens our eyes to the eternal light, our ears to the divine word, and our lips to songs of praise, to the prayer of forgiveness, of petition and of thanksgiving, which are all but different forms of adoration, that is of the homage of the creature before the almighty and all-good God. In the sacrament of confirmation the Blood of Christ strengthens the fighter for the brave profession of his faith. But above all it is the sacrament in which Christ Himself is present, that makes us members of His Body. By taking part in the sacrifice and in the sacrificial meal we are nourished with the Flesh and Blood of Jesus and thus ourselves become His flesh and blood. And His Spirit can quicken and govern us only if and insofar as we are members of His Body: "It is the Spirit that quickens; for the Spirit gives life to the members. Yet He does this only to those that He finds in just that Body which the Spirit quickens . . . Hence the Christian should fear nothing so much as to be separated from the Body of Christ. For if he is separated from the Body of Christ he is no longer His member: if he is no longer His member, he is no longer quickened by His Spirit".* Now we become members of

* St. Augustine, tract 27 in John, lessons 8 and 9 read in the Roman Breviary on the third day of Corpus Christi.

the Body of Christ "not only through love, . . . but in all reality by becoming one with His Flesh; for this is effected by the food He has given us, in order to prove to us His longing for us. Therefore He has Himself penetrated us with His Body that we might become one, as the body is united to its head . . ."* As members of His Body, endowed with His Spirit, we offer ourselves in sacrifice "by him, and with him, and in him", joining our voices to the eternal thanksgiving. Therefore, after receiving the sacred Food, the Church, in the Postcommunion prayer of the first Sunday after Pentecost, puts these words on our lips: "Grant, we beseech thee, O Lord, that, filled with so great gifts, we may both receive graces for our salvation and may never cease from thy praise".

* St. John Chrysostom, Homily 61 to the people of Antioch, *ibid.* lesson 4.

C. THE SPIRIT OF ST. ELIZABETH
OF HUNGARY

The story of the Hungarian princess Elizabeth reads like a wondrous fairy tale. She was born in a castle at Pressburg, while in the same hour the magician Klingsor at Eisenach read her birth in the stars and predicted her future glory and her importance for the land of Thuringia. The descriptions of the treasures which Queen Gertrude collected for the future dowry of her daughter read as if they were taken from *A Thousand and One Nights*, and no less magnificent were the carriages on which they were loaded when the landgrave Hermann of Thuringia had the four year old princess fetched to the distant Wartburg to be betrothed to his son. The queen promised to send still more later, for the actual marriage. But her restless thirst for riches, power and glory came to a sudden end; she was murdered by conspirators, and her child, whom she had sent abroad to secure her a crown, was a motherless orphan. The story of the two children Ludwig and Elizabeth reads like a tender German folk-tale: they grew up together, loving each other like brother and sister and standing by each other, unswervingly faithful when people conspired to separate them. Later all turned away from the strange child who would rather look after beggars in rags than take part in gay festivities, and who seemed to be better fitted for the cloister than for the throne; for she had no inclination to become the centre of a luxurious court life to which the Thuringian knights were accustomed since the days Landgrave Hermann had resided in the Wartburg.

Then follows the knightly romance, the accolade of the young landgrave and his accession, the splendid wedding and the early married happiness of the princely couple, Elizabeth's life as a sovereign by the side of her husband: festivities, hunts, journeys on horseback all through her lands, and in between her quiet care for the poor and the sick around the Wartburg. Then the troubles of a sovereign began to increase: While her husband was away in a war, exposed to danger, she had to be regent in his place and to struggle against famine and epidemics afflicting the people, as well as against the resistance of her entourage, who would not allow her to relieve the distress by all the means at her disposal. Finally Ludwig took the vow to join the Crusade, and her passionate grief at the separation was soon to be followed by the despair of the broken-hearted widow when she received the news of his death. It was, so it seems, a woman's destiny like many others.

But what follows is something new and unparalleled. The widow who had been stricken with grief arises as the 'strong woman' praised by the liturgy of her feast, and takes control of her life. One stormy night she leaves the Wartburg, where she is no longer allowed to live as her conscience bids her. She seeks a refuge for herself and her children at Eisenach, and as she finds no tolerable home there, she accepts for a time the hospitality of her maternal relations. Even when she has been reconciled to the brothers of her husband and has been brought back to the Wartburg with honour and love, she cannot bear it there for long. She must go to the end the way that has opened before her; she must leave her place on the heights to live with the poorest of the poor as one of them; she must entrust her children to strangers, so that she herself may belong only to the Lord to serve Him in His suffering members. Stripped of everything, she vows herself to Him who gave all for His own. On Good Friday of the year 1299 she places her hands on the stripped altar of the church of the Franciscans at Marburg and takes the habit of their Order, to which she had already belonged for years as a Tertiary, without having been able to follow her heart's desire and live entirely in its spirit. Now she is the sister of the poor and serves them in the hospice she had built for them; not for very long, however, for after no more than two years her strength was exhausted, and at the age of twenty-four she was allowed to enter into the joy of her Lord.

It is a life sufficiently colourful and attractive by its external events to charm the imagination and rouse astonished admiration. But we are not concerned with this. We would like to penetrate to what lies behind these external facts; we would wish to feel the beating of this heart that bore such destiny and did such deeds, and to make our own the spirit that animated it. All the facts, all the words reported of Elizabeth reveal her ardent heart, whose gently clinging, faithful love embraced all who approached it. Thus the small hand of the child was placed into that of the boy whom the political ambition of her parents had given her as a companion, never to let it go. Thus she shared her whole life with the playmates given her in her earliest childhood, until her austere spiritual guide removed them from her shortly before her death, to dissolve the last bonds of earthly love. Thus she bore in her heart the children to whom she gave birth when she herself was as yet hardly more than a child. And when she separated from them she surely did it in motherly love which did not want them to share her own hard way, from a sense of duty that would not arbitrarily change their natural destiny; but perhaps also because she felt that her overwhelming love for them was a hindrance to her divinely given vocation.

From her earliest youth she had opened her heart in burning, merciful love to all those in need and distress. She felt urged to feed the hungry and to nurse the sick; but it was never enough for her to alleviate only material needs, she always longed to warm cold hearts at her own heart. In the hospice, the poor children would run into her arms calling her mother, because they felt that they were met by true motherly love. All these overflowing riches sprang from one inexhaustible fountain, from the love of the Lord who had been near her as long as she could remember. When father and mother parted from her, He went with her into the distant foreign land. When she learned that He dwelt in the chapel of the castle, she was drawn there, away from her child's games, and felt at home there. Here she found comfort when people mocked and reviled her. No one was as faithful as He; therefore she, too, must be faithful to Him and love Him above all. No man's image was allowed to oust His image from her heart. Therefore she was overcome with remorse when the consecration bell startled her into the realization that her eyes and heart were turned to the husband at her side instead of following the holy sacrifice. Before the image of the Crucified hanging naked and bleeding on the Cross she could not wear her crown and ornaments. He had extended His arms to draw to Himself all those that labour and are burdenend. Hence she must bring the love of Him to all of them, and awake in them in turn their love for the Crucified. For they were all members of the mystical Body of Christ. By serving them she served the Lord. But she had also to see to it that through faith and charity they would become His living members. She strove to lead to the Lord all those that approached her, thus exercizing a fruitful apostolate. This is proved by the lives of her companions; the development of her husband, too, bears eloquent testimony, as does the inner change of his brother Conrad who, evidently under her influence, became a religious after her death. The spirit that filled and formed the life of Elizabeth was the love of Christ, from which sprang her ever-active charity.

Another of her characteristics springs from the same source: her gaiety that won her so many hearts. She loved wild children's games and still took pleasure in them when, according to contemporary ideas of behaviour, she ought long to have outgrown them. She loved beautiful things and knew how to adorn herself, to arrange brilliant festivities and to entertain her guests when her position demanded this. But she wanted to bring joy especially into the homes of the poor. She took toys to their children and played with them herself. Even the gloomy widow with whom she had to share house in the last period of her life could not diminish her gaiety and had even to bear with her jokes. And she was moved to the depths of her heart on that day when she invited thousands of poor people to come to Marburg, where she distributed with her own hands the remainder of her widow's allowance which was paid to her in cash. From morning to night she had been walking through rows upon rows of them to give everyone his share. At nightfall many had remained who were too old and too weak to make their way home. They camped in the open, and when Elizabeth had fires lit for them, they were so contented that they began to sing. The princess heard it with surprise and found her life-long belief confirmed: "See, I have told you, one need only make the poor happy". She had long been convinced that God had created His creatures for joy and that it was right to show Him a radiant face. This, too, was confirmed to her, when dying, she was called to eternal joy by the sweet song of a bird.

Overflowing love and joy showed themselves in her free natural manner that would not fit into conventions. How could one walk with mincing steps and lisp polite, ready-made little phrases when outside, before the gates the signal was sounded that announced the master's return? Elizabeth would invariably forget all the rules of behaviour when her heart began to beat violently, and she followed its rhythm. Or should one even remember in church in what forms it was socially permitted to express one's devotion? She could not refuse to do what love bade her, even if she was severely reprimanded for it. She could never understand why it should be improper for her to carry gifts to the poor in person, to talk kindly to them, to go into their huts and to care for them in her own home. She did not want to be self-willed and diso- bedient, she had no desire to quarrel with her household, but human voices could not drown the peremptory voice in her heart. Hence she could not continue to live among those who were mesmerized by convention, who neither could nor would break loose from old customs and deep-rooted ideas. She could resign herself to it as long as she was held by a sacred bond and had a faithful protector by her side, who understood the desires of her heart, while at the same time prudently taking account of the needs of others. After her husband's death she felt impelled to leave the circles in which she had been born and brought up in order to go her own way. It was a sharp cut, painful certainly also for her. But in the love of her heart, which would stop before no barriers that separated her from her suffering brothers and sisters, she found the way to the heart of the poor, which today so many seek in vain, though they have the best intentions and spare no effort.

Throughout the centuries men have had a longing that will never come to rest and expresses itself sometimes quietly, at others more loudly. Rousseau, who felt it particularly strongly, found a stirring catchword for it: "Back to nature". And the German poet Heinrich von Kleist, who longingly chased this ideal in vain throughout his life until he broke down, has traced a strangely compelling picture of the man whose whole behaviour flows in unbroken movement from his inmost depths, guided only by the demands of his heart, without the considerations of reason or the effort of the will. Such a man, he thinks, would have the charm of a marionette.

Does St. Elizabeth correspond to this ideal? The facts we have mentioned, which bear witness to her spontaneous way of acting, seem to favour such a view. But our sources also record other facts, which testify no less clearly to a steely will, to an inexorable fight against her own nature: the lovely, youthful, gay and charmingly natural manner belongs to a severely ascetical saint. She has learned early that it is not without danger to follow unrestrainedly the bent of one's heart. Exaggerated love of her relatives, pride and greed had earned Queen Gertrude the hate of the Hungarian people and prepared for her the sudden violent death by murder. Unbridled passion had led Gertrude's sister Agnes of Meran into an adulterous union with the French king and resulted in the interdict for the whole of France. Ruthless ambition involved Landgrave Hermann in a restless life of quarrels and feuds, and caused him to die excommunicate. And she had sometimes to see even her own husband involved in an unjust struggle for power, and under sentence of excommunication. And was she herself free from these sinister powers in her own breast? No, she knew only too well that it is dangerous to surrender oneself to the guidance of one's heart. When, as a child, Elizabeth had with innocent cunning invented games in which she could run to the chapel or throw herself to the ground to say her prayers in secret, this was certainly due to a powerful attraction of grace in the heart of the child; but perhaps she may also have been vaguely conscious of being in danger of straying from God. This became clearer when, as a young girl, she left a ball after the first dance, saying seriously: one dance is enough for the world; I will give up the others for God. If she rose in the night and knelt to pray, or if she even left her room to let herself be scourged by her maids, this is probably due not only to her general desire for penance and voluntary suffering for the sake of the Lord. She wanted to escape the danger of forgetting God at the side of her beloved husband. Surely Elizabeth's natural sense of beauty must have preferred pretty children to ugly ones, and shrunk from the sight and smell of repulsive wounds. If she always chose just such miserable creatures to nurse herself, this was probably caused not only by her merciful love for these poorest of the poor, but also by her determination to overcome her natural revulsion. Even in her last years Elizabeth still asked the Lord for three things: to despise all earthly riches, to bear humiliations with joy, and to be freed from her inordinate love for her children. She would later tell her maids that all her requests had been granted. But the very fact that she had to pray for them shows that they were against her nature, and that for a long time she had probably to struggle for them in vain.

Elizabeth strove to achieve her aim to make her way of life pleasing to God, not only to herself, by battling against her own nature. Quite consciously and with the same inflexible firmness she also sought to influence her surroundings. As landgravine she opposed the exaggerated display of clothes, and tried to induce the wives of the nobility to give up some of their vanities. When she began to avoid all food that had been procured by unjust means, and hence was often compelled to starve at the richly laden princely table, she found it natural that her faithful companions Guda and Isentrud should share her privations, just as they later followed her into the misery of her voluntary exile and poverty. This carefully observed abstinence from food was a powerful protest against the whole way of life of her entourage. Her increasingly austere habits certainly made the most exacting demands on her husband, who had to look on when she treated herself with the utmost severity, endangering her health, and when she recklessly spent his property, which earned her the opposition of his family and his whole court. It needed heroic self-denial also on his part when she eventually strove to break away from him interiorly, and even complained bitterly of the ties imposed on her by her marriage. One can well understand that the young landgrave, who bore all this lovingly and patiently, and faithfully strove to assist his wife in her struggle for perfection, gained a reputation for sanctity with his people.

At first Elizabeth was probably guided in her quest for perfection by the teaching of the Gospel and the general ascetical practices of her time. Now and again she had a flash of insight which she sought to carry out in practice. She found the ideal for which she was looking as a clearly defined form of life, when the Franciscans came to Germany and Rodiger, who was her guest at the Wartburg, told her about the way of life of the Poor Man of Assisi. Then she suddenly knew exactly what she wanted and for what she had been longing all her life: to be utterly poor, to beg from door to door, no longer to be fettered by any possession or any human bond, free even from her own will, to belong only to the Lord. Landgrave Ludwig could not bring himself to dissolve the matrimonial bond and allow her to leave him; but he was willing to help her to follow a rule of life as far as possible adapted to her ideal. It was probably better that her spiritual guide was not to be a Franciscan, else her impossible desires would never have come to rest, but a man who, while fully understanding her inner aspirations, could yet moderate her excessive zeal by the calm voice of reason.

Such a man was Master Conrad of Marburg, who had been recommended to the landgrave as a suitable director for his wife. Though he was a secular priest, he practised the poverty of a mendicant friar, being extremely severe on himself as well as on others, and completely devoted to the service of God. Thus he traversed Germany preaching the Crusade and fighting for the purity of the faith. In 1225 Elizabeth made a vow of obedience to him and remained under his direction until her death. This was probably the most effective breaking of her own will, that she subjected herself to him and always remained subject to him; for he did not only take up the merciless struggle against her lower nature, which was what she herself desired, but he also directed her love of God and her neighbour into ways different from those she herself would have preferred. He never permitted

54

her to give up all her property, neither before nor after the death of her husband; he objected to her indiscriminate almsgiving which he gradually restricted and at last forbade altogether; he sought to prevent her from nursing contagious diseases—the only point in which Elizabeth did not completely obey him even to the end.

His ideal of perfection was certainly no lower than hers. It was clear to him from the beginning that the person entrusted to his guidance was very holy, and he wanted to do all he could to guide her to the summit of perfection. But his views on the means differed from hers. First of all, he wanted to teach her to strive for the ideal in her own state of life, just as he himself had not thought it necessary to enter the Order to which he belonged as a secular priest. So he allowed her to join the Franciscans as a Tertiary, and interpreted the vows according to her condition. As long as her husband was alive she was to fulfil all the matrimonial duties, but in the case of his death she was not to marry again. She was to live in poverty, but not to throw away her property unreasonably but to administer it sensibly for the sake of the poor. The beginning of this life of poverty was marked by the prohibition from eating any food which had not been acquired by lawful means. According to recent research the carrying out of this command seems to have been the reason why she left the Wartburg after the death of her husband. It has been argued that her brother-in-law, Heinrich Raspe, would no longer allow her to separate herself from the princely table; he suspended her income from her widow's estate in order to break her determination, probably also to put an end to her exaggerated almsgiving. After the extreme poverty and loneliness which she had suffered during this voluntary—or involuntary—exile, she was no longer able to accustom herself to her former way of life. After being reconciled to her husband's family she returned to the Wartburg only for a short time and began at once to discuss with Master Conrad in what form she could best realize her Franciscan ideal. He approved of none of her suggestions, permitting her neither to enter a convent nor to take up a hermit's or a beggar's life. But he could not forbid her to renew her vows and be clothed in the habit of her Order. He also allowed her to live in her town of Marburg, which was his own place of residence. He determined what form her life should take according to his own views, building out of her revenues a hospice at Marburg and assigning to her certain duties in it. It was probably her own idea, though also according to the views of her director, that she should spend nothing of her income on herself, but was to work for her modest livelihood with her own hands by spinning wool for the convent of Altenburg.

According to Master Conrad's view his most difficult and important task was to teach his penitent obedience. It was his sacred conviction that obedience is better than sacrifice, and that perfection cannot be attained without detachment from one's own desires and inclinations. In his zeal that she should reach this goal he even let himself be carried away to corporal punishment when she continued to disobey his orders. Elizabeth herself certainly agreed with him in her heart. This is proved not only by the patience and meekness with which she bore these harsh humiliations. For she would certainly not have given in on such an essential point as the sacrifice of her desired form of life, if she had not been fully convinced of the importance of obedience. She looked on the guide whom she had not chosen herself, but who had been given her, as God's representative. His word made known to her His will more surely than the inclination of her own heart. For in the end this alone matters, to shape one's life according to the will of God. Therefore both fought without mercy against her natural inclinations. Sometimes it was Elizabeth herself who led the way and was only approved by the Master; this happened when she moved to Marburg and separated from her children. Sometimes Conrad commanded and Elizabeth obeyed; thus when he took from her the beloved companions of her youth and replaced them by others who were to share her home, whom she found difficult to endure, and when he increasingly curtailed and eventually altogether forbade her to give alms in person which she enjoyed so much. Only on one point did she not completely obey: apart from her hospital duties she insisted on having in her own small house a sick child suffering from a particularly revolting disease and on nursing it quite by herself. A boy sick with psora was sitting even at her deathbed, as Master Conrad himself wrote to Gregory IX. The Pope had charged him to take care of the widow after the landgrave's death, and immediately after Elizabeth had died her director urged Gregory to have her canonized.

*　　*　　*　　*　　*

The picture we have drawn of the saint and of her way of life seems contradictory. On the one hand there is her lively temperament that follows the movements and intuition of a warm heart filled with love, regardless of her own reflexions or the objections of others. On the other we have seen a vehemently determined will incessantly struggling to restrain her own nature and to force her life into a form received from outside, consciously opposing its firm principles to the inclination of her own heart.

Yet there is one point of view from which the contrasts become comprehensible and eventually merge into a harmony that gives the longing to be 'natural' its true fulfilment. Those who profess their faith in 'undeformed human nature' believe in a formative power in man that works from within, undisturbed by outside pressure, shaping man and his life into a perfectly harmonious whole. But experience refuses to confirm this pleasant belief. It is true, the form is hidden within, but it is entangled in wild-growing webs that hamper its pure development. If we leave our nature to itself, it will tend hither and thither without achieving a clear formation. Now formlessness is not natural. But if we discipline our nature, pruning wild shoots and trying to give it the form we think fit—perhaps a form we have found ready made outside—we may, indeed, sometimes make room for the inner form to work itself out; but it may also happen that we do it violence, so that some unnatural fabrication will take the place of freely developed nature. Our knowledge is piecemeal; if we will and act according to this alone, we cannot create anything perfect; also, we cannot do it for the reason that we are not altogether sure of ourselves, and hence will often faint before the goal is reached. Therefore that fettered inner formative power tends towards a light that will lead it securely, towards a force that will make it free and give it the scope it needs. This is the light and the power of divine grace. Its attraction was strong in the soul of the child Elizabeth. It set it on fire, and the flame of divine love began to rise brightly in it, breaking all coverings and barriers. Then this child placed herself in the hands of the divine Artist. Her will became a willing instrument of His, and led by Him it could begin to tame and prune its own nature, to make a way for the inner form. Thus she could also find an outer form suitable for her, into which she could grow without losing her natural direction. And so she ascended to that perfect humanity which is the pure effect of nature liberated and transformed by the power of grace. When we have reached these heights we may follow without danger the bent of our heart, because it has entered into the divine Heart and beats with Its rhythm. Then the bold words of St. Augustine can become the rule of life: Love and do what thou wilt.

MYSTICAL WRITINGS

A. THE KNOWLEDGE OF GOD

We may distinguish three main spiritual trends which have decisively formed the Western mind throughout the Middle Ages, and have thence descended as a living heritage that still affects our own times. They all presuppose the Scriptural revelation as their unshakeable foundation. These three trends are different ways by which to apprehend the Scriptural content, to appropriate it interiorly, to integrate the divine Word with the products of human effort, and thus to achieve a living whole built up from divine and human wisdom. The effect of these three trends is plainly visible in the work of St. Thomas, and the influence they later had was perhaps furthered more by his writings than by any other's. The trends referred to are Greek thought, especially that of Aristotle, the life work of St. Augustine, and the legacy of the 'Areopagite'. As soon as we mention these names the reader will realize that there can be no question of three strictly separate currents. Both the minds of St. Augustine and of the 'Areopagite' were formed, each in its own way, by Greek philosophy. Their work is the first great attempt at clarification, which was later resumed under their guidance. Hence the influence of these two authors is essentially different from that of the Greek philosophers.

It may cause surprise that we should place the 'Areopagite' side by side with Aristotle and St. Augustine; but this is scarcely exaggerating his influence. Nowadays only a small circle of specialists and a few 'amateurs' seem to be acquainted with the ideas and writings of the 'Areopagite'. But the range of his influence extends much further than knowledge of him, since he dominated Western thought from the ninth to the sixteenth century. The Church had recognized him as an authority from the sixth century onwards, and used him as one of her sources in her fight for orthodoxy. In the literature on him published within the last decades it is constantly affirmed that he owed his great influence mainly to his name. We have so far spoken of him in the present article as the 'Areopagite'. This usage is due to a certain embarrassment of the author. The books under discussion came to light towards the end of the fifth century with the name of Dionysius attached to them; that is, we have no earlier testimony of their existence. The writer did not call himself the 'Areopagite'. But he speaks of St. Paul as his teacher and dedicated his works to a fellow priest Timothy. In some passages he also refers to certain events as if he had been an eye witness; these are generally supposed to be the eclipses at the deaths of Christ and of the blessed Virgin. Moreover, all his letters are addressed to persons bearing names well-known in the apostolic age. Hence it was assumed that the author was none other than the member of the Areopagus whose conversion is recorded in the Acts of the Apostles. Early doubts as to the authorship gradually vanished and came to the fore again only in the age of humanism. But a few decades ago certain peculiarities of the *Areopagitica* were thoroughly analyzed, revealing an intellectual and spiritual environment incompatible with the assumption that the texts originated in the apostolic age. Today the majority of experts hold that the works were written at the end of the fifth century.

The author is usually called 'Pseudo-Dionysius'. The quotation marks so far used with the name 'Areopagite' presumably suffice to indicate that the present writer does not believe the author of the *Areopagitica* to have been the disciple of St. Paul. From now on we will simply call him Dionysius or the Areopagite without fear of misunderstanding. It is not within the scope of the present article to discuss the question of the person hiding under, or speaking in, his name. We cannot determine what the author intended by assuming this name, as long as we do not know his identity.

However this may be, we undoubtedly possess the body of his works, consisting of four long treatises and ten letters. Western libraries contain twenty-five Greek and thirty-two Latin manuscripts of them. How they entered and influenced the intellectual and spiritual life of the Middle Ages can be ascertained with unusual precision. It is, indeed, a legend that the Areopagite was the first bishop of Paris and that he was buried in the Abbey of St. Denis. But it is an historical fact that the writings bearing his name started their victorious career in the Western world from this abbey. It is outside the scope of this article to follow the historical development of their influence. We would rather bring out the importance of these texts by presenting one aspect of the peculiar intellectual and spiritual world envisaged in them. This point of view may be of interest to the philosopher as well as to the theologian.

One leading idea runs through all the extant writings of Dionysius; to express it St. Albert the Great used the words of Ecclesiastes: "Unto the place from whence the rivers come they return, to flow again". (1 : 7). This refers in the first place to the order of being; every being proceeds from God who is the First and returns to Him. That they 'flow again' after being reunited to Him does not mean that they are once more separated, but that they incline towards that which is lower, so as to lead it upwards in its turn. This implies a further fundamental feature of the Dionysian conception of the world, namely the order of degrees or steps he calls hierarchy. In his *Ecclesiastical Hierarchies* he defines this as "the whole order of the holy things subjected to it". (1.3). It is to lead all creatures back to their Creator. Like the law of procession and return of which it is part, the hierarchy is not only an order of being but also one of knowledge. A ray proceeds from the inaccessible light which, by its brilliant splendour, veils the First Being to the eyes of creatures. It first falls on the beings closest to Him in the created order, that is the pure spirits. It illuminates them and is passed on from them diffracted to the lower orders, down to the last still capable of being illuminated. This applies in a certain sense to all beings whatsoever. Not all creatures, it is true, can be divinely illumined in such a way as to become capable of knowing God and freely tending towards Him. This is possible only to created spirits, that is angels and men. But even the lowest creatures that are devoid of reason and life may serve as instruments and symbols of the divine Being and its operation. Thus far they are also part of the hierarchical order of being and knowledge, hence are mentioned in the Dionysian treatises on the Celestial and the Ecclesiastical Hierarchies. But only the heavenly spirits and the ordained members of the Church are 'bearers' of the hierarchical functions, being God's messengers that carry the divine light through creation.

In the following we will discuss in greater detail one particular aspect of the wider complex that has just been outlined. It is the doctrine contained in the Dionysian texts on the knowledge of God, which is, indeed, the only form of knowledge in which the author is really interested. It is briefly treated in his work on *Mystical Theology*. This small treatise of only a few pages is nevertheless very important, in view of its contents as well as of the immense influence it was to exercize. Dionysius owes his title of 'Father of Mystics' to this short work, which must not, however, be thought to be a treatise on mysticism or a theory of it in the modern sense. In order to avoid this misunderstanding from the beginning, we must realize what the Areopagite means by the term 'theology', which he does not use in the sense of a science or a systematic doctrine about God. Students of his works emphasize that by 'theology' he means the Scriptures, the Word of God, and by 'theologians' the sacred authors. This is undoubtedly true; even a superficial reader of Dionysius will soon realize that the terms are mostly employed in this sense. Yet this interpretation would not seem to do full justice to the texts. The very title 'Mystical Theology' points to the essential meaning; for, as will be seen presently, it no longer refers to a *speaking* about God. By applying the term 'theologian' to a Daniel, Ezechiel or St. Peter, Dionysius intends to convey not only that these men are the authors of the books or letters bearing their names, but also that they are *inspired* (according to our terminology), and that they speak of God because God has seized them, or God speaks through them. In this sense the angels, too, are theologians, and Christ is the highest of all theologians, because He is the living Word of God. Finally we reach a stage when God Himself will be called the First Theologian. Hence the different theologies distinguished in the treatise on Mystical Theology are not 'disciplines' or branches of this science, but different ways of speaking of God and the different modes of the knowledge of God (or of our lack of knowledge) which they express. Mystical theology is the highest degree of this knowledge. The best translation of the term would perhaps be 'secret revelation'. God is known only if He reveals Himself, and the spirits to whom He does so pass on this revelation. Knowledge and revelation go together. The higher, however, the degree of knowledge, the more obscure and mysterious it becomes, the less will it be possible to express it in words. The ascent to God is made in darkness and silence, the image being taken from the Exodus account (ch. 19) of Moses ascending Mount Sinai, which Dionysius interprets in a mystical sense, in harmony with the general Patristic tradition. While a person is as yet at the foot of the mountain, he may still be able to express his experience fairly adequately. Dionysius himself used such terms in his works that are devoted to positive (as opposed to negative, not in the modern sense of opposed to speculative) theology, such as his treatises on the principal truths of faith, especially the doctrine of the Trinity and the Incarnation. These matters he alleged to have discussed in his 'Fundamental Theology', a work no longer extant, and which most critics believe to be fictitious. These 'positive' terms are also used in his treatise on the Divine Names, where the latter are taken from the purely spiritual sphere.

In 'Symbolic Theology', on the other hand, he asserts to have studied the names applied to divine things that are taken from the sensible world. This treatise, too, is no longer extant. He expounds the mysteries of the Trinity and the Incarnation in the second chapter of his work on the Divine Names, where he distinguishes the 'theology of difference' from the 'theology of unity'. The former deals with the properties of the divine Persons, the latter with the attributes of the Godhead as a whole. Longer discussions of symbolic theology as here understood are contained in the second and the fifteenth chapters of the *Celestial Hierarchies,* and in the ninth letter, which is addresed to Titus. A detailed statement is found in the *Divine Names* chapter three, section five.

The approach from the sensible world is the lowest and allows for breadth. Dionysius affirms that the mind relaxes when it descends in the celestial hierarchies from the purely spiritual vision "into the wider sphere of manifold forms of diverse kinds" that is to the level of angels. The simpler the object—and the simpler the more spiritual it is—the wider the range to be embraced by one glance. For this spiritual view the minds needs a greater effort of concentration than for considering the sensible world, and the brief words used to express it also contain a greater wealth of meaning. Consequently, the treatises on Fundamental Theology and on the Divine Names could be shorter than that on Symbolic Theology. Now, however, on the level of 'mystical theology', we shall "meet, in the immersion into the darkness that is above all comprehension, not only poverty of words, but a total lack of words and of understanding".

The way that leads to this knowledge is the way of negation; it approaches God by denying what He is not. This is also an ascent, since it starts at the lowest level. Positive theology uses the opposite procedure. In positive theology one must begin with what is more closely related to its object in order to assert anything at all about what is fundamentally beyond all positive assertions. God is, indeed, life or goodness in a higher sense than He is air or stone. Negative theology, on the contrary, must start with things most distant from Him. According to this it is true in a higher sense that He is not drunk or angry than that He is not known or named. Negative theology ascends the ladder of created things to ascertain on each of its rungs that the Creator is not to be found there. It goes further, examining all the names positive theology attributes to Him, and is compelled to declare that the meaning of these names fails to describe Him who is above all meaning. In the end negative theology is forced to destroy itself, since negation applies to Him as little as affirmation. "And if we affirm or deny anything of that which comes after Him, we neither affirm nor deny Him, because He is above all affirmation as the perfect and unique cause of all things, and above all negation as the supereminence of that which is simply absolute (in the literal sense, i.e. 'detached from everything'), and above and beyond everything". When the ascent has been achieved, both positive and negative theology cede to mystical theology, which, in its turn, ends in complete silence and union with the ineffable. Positive and negative theology are steps leading up to the summit of the mountain. At first sight they seem to be two different ways of forming a concept of the Creator, both starting from creation. Their opposition, however, proves not to be exclusive. They complement each other on each of the steps. Positive theology rests on the analogy of being between the Creator and the creature, the *analogia entis*, as St. Thomas says, following Aristotle. Negative theology is based on the fact that beside the 'similarity' there exists a 'greater dissimilarity', as St. Thomas never wearies to point out. Both theologies meet at the summit of 'mystical theology', where God Himself unveils His mysteries, while at the same time showing us that they are impenetrable.

*

Dionysius lists 'symbolic theology' as the lowest degree of positive theology. As has been said before, he often refers to a book dealing especially with this subject, but this is no longer extant. Hence his concept of symbolic theology has to be construed from relevant passages scattered in the text of the works at our disposal.

The most explicit statement is in the ninth letter addressed to Titus. According to this, the mysterious truth that is beyond the grasp of the uninitiated has been presented by the sacred authors in images that have to be solved like riddles. In the same way the eternal Truth, which is the very fount of life, hides Itself in the divine mysteries, i.e. in the Eucharist, under the veil of sensible shapes. In order to avoid crude misunderstanding, such image language needs to be interpreted; else phrases such as 'God's womb' from which the Son proceeds, the 'breath of His mouth', God's 'wrath', 'ebriety' or 'sleep' might be taken in their literal sense. Holy Scripture is full of such images that might well scandalize people lacking proper understanding. But if we are able to see the beauty hidden under the image we shall find it full of light and revealing God. These metaphorical expressions are meant to conceal what is holy from the desecrating eyes of the crowd and to reveal it to those who strive for holiness; for having freed themselves from childish habits of thought, they have obtained the lucidity of mind that is needed for contemplating simple truths. Thus all the teachers of the Old and the New Covenant have preached God through suitable images; the angels, too, have revealed divine things under mysterious signs. Jesus Himself spoke in parables and instituted the Blessed Sacrament in the image of the Supper. This way of attaining to the light of the divine nature is suited to the human nature. For our life is, indeed, both divided and undivided. That part of the soul which does not need sensible impressions might be destined for the simple interior contemplation of divine images; on the other hand, it is right for that part of the soul which needs impressions that it should be raised to divine things by types and symbols. According to the words of St. Paul (the reference is probably to Rom. 1:20) the whole visible creation represents the invisible essence of God. Therefore the sacred authors described some things only with reference to civic relations and laws, others in their spiritual purity, some in a human way, others supernaturally and perfectly. In order to understand these images we have to rise above the customary interpretation and try to penetrate their meaning in a way that befits sacred things. Thus the image of 'fire', for example, is used in Scripture not only for God Himself, but also for His word and for the heavenly spirits, though not in each case in the same sense. Another explanation is given not in this text but in the *Celestial Hierarchies*. (Ch. 15). When speaking of the angels the author refers to wheels and living beings made of fire, men shining like fire, heaps of glowing coals, and streams of fire flowing with a mighty noise. The Thrones are called fiery, and the name of the Seraphim is interpreted as "the burning ones". This image is preferred for expressing the similarity between the heavenly spirits and God; that it should be used so frequently for God Himself is probably due to the fact that fire has many properties apt to represent the divine essence.

"The sensible fire is, if one may say so, inside all things, passing though all of them, yet remaining pure in itself, and is received by all things. Though it is wholly luminous, it is at the same time also hidden. It remains unknown unless it meets some substance in which it can manifest its power. It can neither be measured nor can one look into it. It dominates and governs all wherein it is to achieve its proper work. It can change things and let whatever comes near it participate in its nature. It renews everything by its living warmth and enlightens by its brilliant illuminations . . . it has a decomposing power without being changed itself. It mounts upward and is penetrating . . . Moving incessantly, it moves itself and other things; it comprises others, yet is never comprised by them. It has no need of anything, it reveals the greatness of its being in whatever is capable of receiving it . . . However much it communicates itself by illuminating, it is never diminished". This description of fire shares unmistakeable traits with statements of the divine Wisdom (cf. Wisdom 7: 22ff.); the ways of speaking in images and without them explain each other.

Another image, that of the mixing bowl, also seems to be taken from the Wisdom literature; Dionysius comments it in the ninth letter (cf. Prov. 9: 2f.). "The Scriptures say of the beneficent Wisdom that it sets up a mystic mixing bowl, pouring into it a holy liquid; but first it has set up solid food and, raising its voice, has kindly invited all in need of it. Divine Wisdom thus dispenses two kinds of food, one solid and durable, the other liquid, meant to be poured out. Its goodness which cares for all beings is dispensed by means of this mixing bowl; it is round and open, to signify the all-embracing Providence which penetrates and comprises all things. Though attaining all things, it remains within itself, always the same, stable and immovable, just as the mixing bowl is solid and firm. Now it is said that Wisdom builds herself a house and there serves solid food, providing cups and the mixing bowl. By this those who meditate divine things fittingly, will understand that Wisdom always and for ever originates both being and well-being. It goes forth to everything, unfolding in the universe and surrounding all things. And He who originates is at the same time in an eminent sense within Himself and in no way whatever in any of the things. He is separated from all and the same in Himself in the same manner, being and subsisting eternally, always behaving in the same way. He never goes forth from Himself, leaving His proper seat of His immovable dwelling and His homestead. Rather, staying within, Wisdom performs the whole and perfect work of Providence, going forth towards everything and remaining within at the same time, standing and moving, yet not standing and moving, permanently possessing, as it were, the power of exercizing its Providence in such a way as to remain stable in exercizing it, in a manner both fitting and transcending nature". (9, 1,3).

"But what is solid and what is liquid food? It is, indeed, said that beneficent Wisdom dispenses and provides both. The solid food signifies, I suppose, an intellectual and lasting perfection. Thus the mental powers of those to whom the divine Paul, drawing from the well of Wisdom, gives a share in the truly solid food, are able to participate in the divine with a steady, powerful, unified and indivisible knowledge. The liquid food, on the other hand, signifies, as I see it, the doctrine which, spreading and flowing forth, tends to pass beyond everything, leading its disciples by means adapted to their capacities, through what is manifold, diverse and divided, to the simple and undivided knowledge of God. For this reason the spiritual words of God are compared to dew and water, or to milk, wine and honey, because, like water, they have the power to bring forth life; like milk, they further growth, they revive like wine and heal and preserve like honey. This divine Wisdom gives its followers, providing them with abundant plenty and inexhaustible joy. This means truly to be fed, and therefore it is said that Wisdom brings forth and feeds, revives and perfects men". (ibid. 4).

Dionysius uses a kindred way of expression when he refers to the 'drunkenness' *(ebrietas)* of God to indicate the ineffable superabundance of goodness which exists in Him as its origin, before being poured out. The insensibility which characterizes this state must be referred to the eminence of God transcending all sense, to the fact that He is above all knowing and being known, even above all being. Similarly the banquets of the saints in the kingdom of heaven signify the harmonious communion of saints participating in the divine goodness and the plenitude of the good things they enjoy. Their victory means that they rest from all their labours; their life has become invulnerable; they are moving in the light and in the land of the living, since Jesus gladdens their heart, gives to each his place at table, serves them in person and lavishes on them the fullness of all goodness. (Cf. ibid. 5).

At the end of the letter Dionysius briefly explains God's 'sleeping' and 'awakening'. Divine sleep signifies His transcendence and the impossibility for the objects of His Providence to communicate with Him. His waking is interpreted as the attention He gives to those who need to be educated and saved.

In a passage of another work Dionysius attempts to clarify the mode of expression that characterizes 'symbolic theology'. He shows that the human mind seeks to understand the invisible through the visible also in the sphere of created things. Although the soul is strictly indivisible, it may be represented as having parts, after the manner of bodily shapes. If such expressions be used the 'parts' will have a different meaning from that referring to bodies. The faculty of intellectual knowledge may be called the head; opinion, being midway between reason and unreason, may be called the neck, and so forth. This means that the names of parts of the body may be used as symbols for the powers of the soul. We may thus also speak of God's breadth, length or depth, in order to indicate His going forth to all things, His power over them, and the fact that He is hidden and cannot be known by creatures.

*

We will try in the following paragraphs to discover the meaning of 'symbolic theology' on the basis of the fragments just discussed. According to a brief reference in the *Mystical Theology* (ch.3) the problem is how to apply the names of sensible things to what is divine. We shall examine what these sensible things are, to what their names are applied, and in what sense this 'transfer' of names should be understood. Finally we shall have to ask what kind of relationship between the things signified directly and those signified indirectly is actually presupposed both by the speaker and by his hearers.

The passage referred to above lists a long series of such 'transfers': forms, shapes, parts, tools, places, ornaments, passion, grief and anger, drunkenness and irritation, oaths, sleep and waking. Some of them appeared in the preceding examples. They are partly objects of sense perception, things and properties of things, such as the mixing bowl, the forms of bread and wine, spatial extension or fire; partly bodily and mental states and processes such as sleep and waking, drunkenness, anger and the like, or social acts such as oaths and curses, and events. as in the case of the wedding feasts and other instances mentioned in the parables of Scripture.

Symbolic language, therefore, takes its terms from the spheres of exterior and interior experience as well as from what may be called the 'experience of life' that is formed by an agglomeration of diverse elements. The term 'sensible things' must be taken in a strict sense. It obviously refers to all we experience in our daily life either directly or through mental images arising in our mind whenever things are mentioned by name. In symbolic language these names are used to signify something other than what we know in our daily experience. The Areopagite calls that to which these names are transferred 'the divine'. He uses this term in a very large sense, so that it has various meanings. This is clear from the way he uses it elsewhere. He applies it not only to God Himself and to everything related to His being or to the Sacraments instituted by Him (the 'divine mysteries'), but he calls divine also the angels and certain human beings, especially bishops. He speaks of divine joy in connexion with the consecration of monks and so forth. The term occurs on almost every page. It is one of his favourite expressions that characterizes his style. The examples also show that fire is an image of God Himself, of His word. and of the angels. The mixing bowl is a symbol of divine providence, food and drink are images of various forms of instruction insofar as it arises from participating in the divine Wisdom; they are also the forms in which the Godman offers Himself in a hidden manner. In the latter instance the symbol is no longer the 'name', but the visible forms that are actually present, having not only an intelligible meaning but also a present reality. This latter, however, has to do with the relation between the symbol and that which it indicates. For the moment we are concerned with the goal to which symbolic theology would lead us through the images that are taken from the world of experience. This is in itself manifold and may perhaps be covered by the term kingdom of God. Its *raison d'être* and its dominating centre is God Himself. He is the true and ultimate goal with which symbolic theology is concerned. The effects that proceed from Him and penetrate into the created world preserve something of His essence; hence they are 'divine' and divinize everything that receives them. No more than God Himself can we handle or see with our bodily eyes these 'emanations' of the divine essence, that is to say all that is alive in creatures, being in His likeness and capable of being united to Him in the unity of His kingdom. Hence these 'divine things' must be suggested to human beings confined to the world of natural experience by images taken from this world, the only one they know.

How does such image-language become possible? In other words, what are the actual conditions allowing this language to be spoken and understood? To make this clear we have first to ask what is the particular sense in which the word image is used in the present context. The preceding remarks suggest that here, too, we should not expect an unequivocal answer. It seems best once more to begin with the terms used by Dionysius himself. He concludes the list of images mentioned above with the succinct summary: "And as many other sacredly shaped forms of symbolic representations of God as there may be".

As regards the term symbol it should be realized that the image-relation is not necessarily implied in the original meaning. The notion of 'throwing together'* has assumed different meanings in Greek terminology. Those most closely related to the problems under discussion may be comprised under the heading 'mark by which something may be recognized'. In this sense the Christians called their creeds 'symbols', as a means of recognizing

* The original meaning of the Greek word symbol. Ed.

73

each other. The term means further 'characteristic' and lastly 'sign'. We gather from other expressions used in this context that the symbol must be considered as an 'image'. As regards this, we are told that it concerns something formed or shaped by someone in the way an artist shapes his work (this is implied in the terms *typos* and *plastós*); hence it is a 'formation' *(mórphosis)* to be apprehended by the senses, and it is related to God as an idea to its realization or an image to the original.*

The concept of what is formed or shaped can also mean two things: it refers on the one hand to what 'theology' presents to us, that is to the words used by the Scriptures when speaking of God or of divine things; on the other hand to that which these words express, i.e. the things they name, such as the fire or the mixing bowl. the events reported, as in the parables, or the actions by which the prophets would present their message to the senses. Christ, too, revealed divine truth not only by His words but by His actions, and the Church teaches through her liturgical ceremonies.

It would be interesting to examine how words can conjure up an image before our eyes and at the same time make it point beyond itself to something indirectly expressed by these words, which the image is meant to represent. This question, however, is outside the scope of the present discussion. We would rather try to understand the image-relation that exists between what is directly and indirectly expressed by the words. When Moses says: "The Lord thy God is a consuming fire, a jealous God" (Deut. 4:24) he is in a definite sense the 'theologian' who forms and shapes. Like a magician he conjures up before our eyes the image of fire. He 'forms' it, because he apprehends it in a certain way, seeing it under a particular aspect, namely as a 'consuming fire' The terms 'forming' or 'shaping' do not imply anything arbitrary in this context. They should rather be taken to mean that he shaped the image in this particular way, because it so shaped

* The German expressions here and elsewhere indicate an inner relationship which is lost in translation. *Bilden* (to form), *Gebilde* (that which is formed), *Bild* (image), *einbilden* (impress a form) and *Urbild* (original) all share the root. R. Allers.   Such terminological analyses are a characteristic of E. Stein's philosophical works.   Ed.

itself 'in him'. It imposed itself on his mind as an image of God, because he experienced Him like this. There was a similarity between the ineffable Godhead he encountered and the 'consuming fire'; both had a common trait. In this instance there exists an image-relation in the proper sense. Something we meet in the sphere of sense experience represents something else, because both have common characteristics that allow the latter to be recognized in the former. The particular fact that the thing represented can never become an object of sense experience is not necessarily implied in the image-relation as such, but is peculiar to an image of God. But the possibility of recognizing the thing represented by looking at the image belongs to the image as such, hence also to the image of God.

*

In order to use something as an image the original must be known. The theologian (always taking this term in the sense of the Areopagite, as one speaking of or announcing God) must know God so as to form images of Him. What, then, is the foundation of this presupposed knowledge of God? There are several sources from which it may be drawn: natural knowledge of God; faith as the 'ordinary' way of supernatural knowledge of God, and finally a supernatural experience of God as the 'extraordinary' way of a supernatural knowledge of God.

The study of Dionysius' writings does not give the impression that the author considered natural knowledge a possible source of his theology. Indeed, whether or not he thought such a knowledge at all possible is a question difficult to answer on the basis of his work. Most passages read as if he wanted to exclude natural knowledge as dangerous, although he does not seem to think it altogether impossible. In present-day terminology natural theology refers to a doctrine of God developed by natural reason from natural experience. Its nucleus is the proofs of the existence of God and the doctrine of God's nature and properties that can be deduced from our knowledge of the created world. This doctrine proceeds by conceptual thought and discursive reasoning necessarily based on sensible data. The qualification 'sensible' must be taken in a broad sense, as opposed to conceptual thought which presupposes certain data. In this sense the term covers all sensible as well as intellectual experiences, and within the former things actually present as well as those represented.

To make scientific thought possible, there must be a primary intuition supplied by the external senses. The external world is presented to the human eye by this intuitive evidence, hence much more is apprehended than what strictly affects the senses. In more than one respect perception always surpasses what affects the senses. Together with the immediately apprehended material something else is given in union with it, namely all that which does not actually affect the senses at the moment, but which could do so in principle, which may be apprehended when perception progresses. This mode of 'givenness' may be characterized as 'empty intuitive' *(leer-anschaulich)*. But many features are given simultaneously which can never affect the senses or be attained by sense perception.

*

Here we have to mention first the inner structure of spatial and corporeal nature and the laws governing it; aspects which mathematical science attempts to apprehend by its own proper concepts. To give just one example. We perceive causation, though it can never become an object of sense perception as such. Sense perception apprehends the world as something real; this is presupposed by all inquiry into the laws of causality. The scientist follows the lines of inquiry traced by such implications, disregarding others that are equally present. This disregard is essential to the scientist's concept of nature, which is abstract if compared with the fullness of the world that is apprehended by the senses.

Seen in this fullness, the world still has another 'interior' apart from that studied by science. Among the impressions our senses convey, we come across the difference between animate and inanimate beings. Life and soul are apprehended simultaneously (together with the other sense impressions), in external perception, but, strictly speaking, they are never seen from outside.

Nevertheless, they are truly experienced 'from within'. And what is apprehended together with, and implied in, the external world, can be harmonized, as it were, with what we experience in ourselves.

Even apart from the particular characteristics of beings endowed with life or soul, the plenitude of the world perceived by the senses contains more than can be grasped by the methods of science. This world is 'our world', in which we experience love and joy, which we face with delight or admiration, with awe or with horror. It is a whole full of meaning, which speaks to us in a thousand voices, revealing its being as a whole and in every one of its parts, yet remaining a mystery for ever. And through all it manifests and conceals, this world points beyond itself to Him who mysteriously reveals Himself through it. This world with its implied suggestions that point beyond it forms the visible basis for the demonstrations of natural theology. It is also the ground from which springs the language of images, the recognition of values and at the same time the understanding of 'symbolic theology'. The Psalmist hears the voice of God in nature. Yet he does not know God only from this course. Rather, he finds God in all things, because he has faith, and God's voice speaks in his soul. Nevertheless, it cannot be denied that some images may be derived directly from nature. "The voice of the Lord is upon the waters" (Ps. 28: 3). It is natural to man to interpret the growling thunder as the manifestation of a higher power. Hence the image of 'God's voice' is suggested and can safely be assumed to be generally intelligible. In this instance, symbolic language expresses real or assumed knowledge. Where this exists, the image does more than merely represent something previously known but not actually remembered, causing recognition of what is represented by the image. It will also induce knowledge of something not yet known. The 'theologian' comes to know God through the image; so the image is not the work of the theologian, but of God. God has revealed or mirrored Himself in His work, and lets Himself be known thereby. Though He was not known before and hence cannot be 'recognized', the concept of the image as a 'reproduction' is not meaningless. For through a portrait we may not only recognize an acquaintance, but also become acquainted with someone we do not know. If we look at it we also know that it is a *portrait* and that it is a good one. This is actually possible, though it can be realized only if the person who looks at it possesses the 'sense' for it and the necessary training of the eye. What is nowadays called a 'symbol' would seem to be most perfectly realized when a visible form is apprehended as an 'image with a meaning' *(Sinn-Bild)*, revealing something hitherto unknown.

Hence God Himself is the first and original theologian. His 'symbolic theology' is coextensive with creation. The theologians of whom Dionysius speaks, the sacred authors, are men who have an original understanding of this natural revelation. They have the gift of understanding the image-relation of God and of translating it into human language, so that they can lead others to God through symbolic theology. We may safely assume that they are 'chosen vessels' by nature, that they possess the faculty we call 'religious sense' in an unusual degree. This sense and the other capacities of these men may be further developed by a particularly favourable natural environment. This, however, must not be taken to mean that natural revelation is accessible only to such chosen people. On the contrary, it is the very sense of their mission that others, too, should be able to find God in this way. Else their image-language would be unintelligible. Their task is only to teach others, so that these, listening to their teachers, may learn to understand nature. (It is well to remember that even sense perception has to be learned, and it is not learned equally well by everyone).

*

Natural knowledge is only one possible basis for understanding symbolic theology and its images. The natural basis, however, is much broader than the reference to the one example we have cited would suggest. We have said before that images are taken not only from exterior, but also from interior experience. When Moses said: "The Lord is a consuming fire", he elucidated the exterior by an interior image. The language of the Psalms was evidently largely shaped by the experience of the divine government, affecting the personal destiny of individuals as much as the course of great historical events. Here, as also in the parables, the sphere of sense perception is definitely abandoned. The image takes on an ideal character, presupposing a spiritual penetration of original experiences on a higher spiritual level. We shall reserve a further discussion of these problems for a future occasion. In this limited framework it is indeed impossible to point out the various possible ways of a natural knowledge of God, to explain their importance for symbolic theology, or to consider their peculiarities and differences. For the present we must be content to state that the natural knowledge of God provides an abundant source on which symbolic theology may draw.

*

It is hardly possible to decide exactly how far the influence of natural knowledge goes, and if it can ever actually be the only source. After all, each of the 'theologians' is firmly grounded in faith. To the authors of the Old Testament, God is first of all the God of Abraham, Isaac and Jacob, the God of their forefathers, whose great deeds they have heard recited from their early youth, in whose service they have been brought up. In this context, therefore, faith has the proper meaning of *fides*, of the acceptance and preservation of supernatural revelation; it is not synonymous with the looser meaning of 'belief'. The term 'supernatural revelation' refers to the self-revelation of God in His words, especially to the revelation of those mysteries that are hidden in Him and inaccessible to natural knowledge. (In the present context those facts contained in revelation that are also naturally knowable may be disregarded.) God's Word is revelation of supernatural truth; addressed to man, it demands faith in the sense of accepting and preserving revealed truth. Faith is rightly called knowledge insofar as it communicates truth. But it is dark knowledge, because the conviction it brings is not based on an understanding of the truth it accepts. If we use the terms 'God's Word' and 'addresses', this does not mean that supernatural revelation always implies a definite and direct speaking of God in a human manner. The words of His messengers, His prophets and apostles that are spoken in His name to those who are called to the faith, are also divine word and address. First of all, this is true of the Scriptures. The sacred authors were 'faithful' in the sense that they led a life of faith before, and continued to do so after they had been called. The higher light they received did not shine steadily; it suddenly elevated them above their ordinary state for a moment, but it left lasting effects in them. Here we are concerned only with the fact that, regardless of all extraordinary illumination, faith itself is a possible source of the image-language of symbolic theology. When the poet who wrote certain Psalms contemplated the destiny of the chosen people as he knew it from sacred history—the marvellous promises and the guidance of divine grace, the ever repeated apostasy of the people and the terrible judgments and punishments—certain images of God may have suggested themselves as it were spontaneously. God was the father of orphans, or the faithful shepherd, on the other hand the angry judge who delivers His people to be killed like sheep, whose wrath is kindled. This language could be understood through the medium of faith; since the people that listened to the Psalms and sang them were living in the same tradition as the sacred singer. He simply gave expression to what was alive in the hearts of his audience, or aroused what was asleep in them.

*

Faith, by which we accept the revealed word of God, ultimately refers back to something other. God speaks through His messenger; if His words are to be received as coming from Him, they must be somehow distinguished from ordinary human words, and those who announce them must prove that they are His messengers. The simple believer is satisfied with the proof supplied by Scripture. It is part of his faith, based on the teaching of the Church, that the Scriptures are God's Word and that the authors of the various books are 'inspired', that is directed by the Spirit of God. It is not within his competence to examine this inspiration, or to ask how this or that word came to be included in the Scriptures. Yet there must be some way to be assured of both. The second question belongs to Biblical criticism and may be disregarded. We can assume that any given passage is genuinely Scriptural, hence must be considered inspired not only by the simple faithful but also by the theologian (in the modern, not the Dionysian sense). Revelation means that God wants to make known something through a particular text. Inspired means that God moved the author to write this down, or possibly, moved a person to speak the words reproduced in the text. It must now be asked whether the inspired person who becomes the instrument of divine revelation must necessarily be aware of this; further, whether he must be aware of having been accorded an illumination, and thirdly, whether he must himself have received a revelation. It is conceivable that nothing like this has occurred. It is not impossible that someone may be speaking words of revelation without realizing it, without having received an actual revelation from God, without being himself borne by God's Spirit as concerns his subject and way of speaking. He may think that he expresses nothing but his own opinion in words of his own choosing. Thus Caiphas spoke in the council of priests and Pharisees: "You know nothing. Neither do you consider that it is expedient for you that one man should die for the people and that the whole nation perish not". And St. John adds: "And this he spoke not of himself; but being the high priest of that year, he prophesied that Jesus should die for the nation". (John 11: 49-51). Hence Caiphas spoke in the name of God and by divine ordinance, without either knowing or willing it. Yet St. John knew that Caiphas spoke God's words. Did he know the prophetic significance of Caiphas' words by a special revelation? This is quite possible. But it is also possible that St. John realized the prophetic character of this utterance when he contemplated the whole work of Redemption, because these words were fulfilled in the death of Jesus.

Normally, however, a man would not become the instrument of divine revelation without knowing and willing it. It may be useful to compare the preceding account with the great vision of

Isaias (ch.6). The prophet sees the Lord sitting on the throne of glory, he speaks to Him from mouth to mouth and receives words he is to transmit to the people. It seems that seeing and hearing must here be taken in a strictly literal sense. The scene the prophet describes should not be understood to be a symbolic description of something contemplated in a purely spiritual manner. Here, too, God Himself is the 'symbolic theologian', revealing Himself, who is incomprehensible, in a visible image and through human words, and having revealed Himself to the man who is standing before Him, charges him with His mission. Isaias is aware both of the revelation and the mission he receives. Thus, when he stands before the people, he knows that his message is strictly the word of God. In this case revelation, inspiration and the consciousness of both are simultaneously present.

The question then arises how the prophet can be certain that he is actually standing before God. Seeing with the eyes or with the imagination is no indispensable condition of this certainty. These traits may be absent, and yet he may be utterly certain that it is God who speaks to him. This certitude may be based on the 'feeling' that God is there; a man feels himself touched by the divine presence in his inmost being. This is called experience of God in the strictest sense. It is the centre of all mystical experience, in which God is met as one person is met by another. This may be accompanied by a sensible vision, as in the case of Isaias, but this is an inessential phenomenon.

On the other hand, can one conceive of such a vision without a true experience of God? It is not impossible for a prophet to see the Lord before Him or to hear His words without being mystically touched by Him in his inner being. This was obviously the case with the boy Samuel, who heard God calling him without realizing that it was God, because he did not recognize Him. Isaias may have been convinced of God's presence without an inner contact with Him, because of the miraculous character of the vision and because the things he saw and heard agreed with what he knew about God by faith. This interpretation cannot be absolutely rejected as impossible; nevertheless, it seems a rather artificial construction. We read of young Samuel that he did not yet know the Lord; this seems to suggest that Eli knew Him, and that Samuel, too, would learn to know Him. We gain the strong impression that Samuel knew the Lord after He had been given the revelation; and this knowledge did not arise from discursive reasoning and intellectual considerations, but from personal contact. Having been touched in his inmost being, the child was transformed into a prophet. We would not claim that this interpretation is the only possible one; but it is possible, and, explained in this way, the event may serve as a useful basis for our theory. In such a true experience of receiving a mission, inspiration, revelation and the consciousness of both are combined with a direct experience of God. Now there are many intermediate degrees between this fullness of experience and the other extreme of a revelation made to a person without his either knowing or consenting to it.

*

To start from below: there may be an inspiration, and the person concerned may be conscious of it, but without receiving any special revelation. The sacred author knows that he is moved by the divine spirit to say or write something, as well as how to express it; he may experience inspiration as such, yet what he has to say bears no relation to his person. It may be an event he knows from experience, or a moral truth which he understands naturally. Such must have been the origin of parts of the historical and Wisdom books. The opposite, however, that is revelation without some type of inspiration, is obviously impossible. Whenever God reveals Himself or a hidden truth, He does it through His Spirit, and whenever a man is chosen to transmit such a truth to others, he must be guided by this Spirit. A mind may be enlightened by divine truth without hearing or seeing anything. The choice of words in which to cast his message may be left to the man himself. If he receives a revelation through audible words or by way of an image, he may only have to pass on this image or these words without himself understanding them. But it is also possible that the spiritual meaning is made clear to him either by an interior illumination or by an added verbal explanation.

In all such cases as have been mentioned above there is more than a mere natural knowledge of God and also something surpassing faith; but there need not always be a personal and experimental knowledge of God. It is open to question where we are allowed in all these cases to speak of a knowledge of God. It seems right to say that any experience endowed with the character of the supernatural is apprehended as coming from God. When divine truth appears in the splendour of a 'supernatural light', that is as clearly distinct from natural knowledge and intruding into the sphere of the latter, this light is seen to be the 'divine light'. If words are heard or a figure is seen, and the one that speaks or appears does not claim to be God Himself but an angel or a saint, he yet comes from God as His messenger. The person receiving the revelation knows that he is under the divine influence, which comes to him through this messenger or through an intellectual vision. (This may be affirmed also of inspiration, unless it be possibly of demonic origin.) But under the conditions just discussed man does not stand before the face of God, nor does God cease to be hidden. Isaias, however, beheld God Himself and heard His words; and if our interpretation of the account is correct, he was certain in his inmost being that God Himself was present. Only when this happens do we have the right to speak of a personal experimental knowledge of God.

This 'feeling of God's presence' has been called above the centre of all mystical experience. It is nevertheless only the beginning, the lowest degree of mystical prayer. There are many steps and transitions between this stage and the summit of infused contemplation, which is permanent union with God. At each higher stage God reveals and gives Himself to the soul more abundantly and deeply; and the soul in its turn penetrates Him more profoundly, this increasing familiarity with Him again demanding its ever more perfect surrender. Personal experimental knowledge has a directness that is lacking in those revelations in which God does not reveal Himself but only an isolated truth or event that cannot be attained by natural knowledge. The difference is similar to that between the direct experience of a thing that is immediately present, and one that is seen only in

84

THE KNOWLEDGE OF GOD

its effects, or made present only through a messenger. But God is never immediately apprehended in the same way as we perceive something with our senses or recognize it as true by spiritual or intellectual insight.

The term 'experience of God' applies in the strictest sense only to a personal encounter. Now the kinds of indirect knowledge referred to above must be counted among the supernatural *experiences*, and thus be distinguished from faith. All kinds of supernatural experience, but personal acquaintance in particular, are related to faith as, on the natural level, personal experience is related to knowledge by hearsay. All kinds of experience fulfil and perfect something that had so far been known only theoretically without being apprehended directly. Personal encounter differs from indirect experimental knowledge in that it brings fulfilment, since the object known as present fulfils what had so far been known only indirectly or by representation. Nevertheless, personal encounter does not yet bring complete fulfilment, but points beyond itself to a truer fulfilment in a higher mystical experience, and, ultimately, in the beatific vision. (We will not here raise the question whether the beatific vision itself is still lacking some perfection, since it is not the vision by which God contemplates Himself).

Compared with the natural knowledge of God, faith is characterized by fulfilment, though not in the way in which personal experience completes what is merely known. The two are related rather in the same way as that which is clearly known is to something only darkly 'guessed'; that is, if we understand by the natural knowledge of God the fact that He appears together with, or in natural experience, so to speak His co-appearance, as of a higher power, but not yet natural theology. We may speak also of materially enriched knowledge, insofar as faith supplies us with new information over and above that gathered from natural experience and natural theology. Finally, we may explain the relationship as that of something previously known which is later confirmed by a higher authority. On the other hand, the transition from natural to supernatural knowledge of God may be compared to becoming personally acquainted with someone whose existence was until then only inferred from certain effects, on the basis of which it was assumed. Faith may provide a bridge for this transition. We may also consider this transition from the natural to the supernatural knowledge of God as happening without the mediation of faith, that is as a gift of grace given to a person till then devoid of faith. If this experience is 'accepted', the various kinds of fulfilment will coexist in this experience, so that the whole event will have the character of an interior revolution and transformation in a much higher degree.

*

All kinds of knowledge of God are connected with each other by the 'intentions', through which they point beyond themselves, and are ultimately directed towards the experience of God. This does not mean that the natural knowledge of God and faith presuppose a supernatural experience preceding them in time, nor that they are justified by such an experience; but that it is part of their proper nature to aim at this and that within this new mode of knowledge they themselves may still be found to exist in a transformed state.

The concept of a supernatural knowledge of God must be cleared up so that we may realize what it can do for 'symbolic theology' (i.e. in the Dionysian sense, as image language about God). Compared with the natural knowledge of God and with faith, inspiration, 'non-personal' revelation and visions may provide new images and at the same time give the certainty that they are fitting perfectly. What the prophet sees and hears forms, as it were, the advanced teaching of symbolic theology. The sacred author is provided with images and words that enable him to express the ineffable and to render the invisible visible. Even more important is the inner contact with God without word or image. In this personal encounter the mind becomes intimately acquainted with God and thus capable of forming a faithful image of the original. On the basis of this experience images and words may come to mind capable of representing God as He had made Himself known. This intimate knowledge also gives the theologian a term of reference or a right instinct when deliberately looking for suitable words and images in which to clothe his experience.

We must once more ask what are the conditions for understanding such an image-language that is drawn from ultimate sources. The answer is that it will be most adequately understood by someone who already possesses such an experimental knowledge of God; for he alone can recognize the God whom he knows personally from His 'portraits'. But faith, too, and even natural knowledge, provide the basis for a certain understanding. If we know and love God, having a living faith, we shall want to know Him from ever new angles and in ever new characteristics, and shall therefore always turn to the Scriptures for more information. Here, too, we have a kind of 'recognizing'. The believer has already an image of God in his mind which he then enriches with the new images in which he finds God represented. Thus he can add new traits to his image, which he then also discovers in the old images. (The term image is here used in several senses. 'My image of God' introduces no duality into the image and what it represents; but the image means God as I know and understand Him). The domain of faith is not abandoned in this process; but there is a progress within faith, clearly distinguishable from a purely natural and rational apprehension of the literal sense, but different also from the experimental knowledge of God. An unbeliever does not become acquainted with *God* by reading the Scriptures, say, as a student of linguistics or of religious history. He will only learn what the Scriptures and those who believe in them *think* about God, unless this reading awakens faith in him; but in this case one attitude would be replaced by another. Even within the sphere of faith itself there are different ways of understanding and of familiarity. A believer will accept all he reads in the Scriptures 'in faith', that is as revealed truth, but this does not necessarily entail that his soul will apprehend it all in a living way. The apprehension may largely remain empty, without influence on experience, and limited to a merely literal understanding. This difference is not the same as the theological distinction between living and dead faith, which refers to the possession or the loss of the state of grace. We become keenly aware of this difference if we suddenly see a Scriptural text in a new light, by which we are shown something hitherto unknown either in God or in our own soul; or the reader may be personally struck by a divine demand he did not realize before, or find that a doctrinal truth hitherto known only in isolation is actually closely related to another. All this is possible 'in the light of faith'. Our knowledge of God is thus enriched, our relation to God deepened or made more harmonious, nevertheless we are not brought face to face with Him. Yet this, too, may happen. A word in Scripture may strike a person in his inmost being, making him feel that God Himself is speaking to him so that he becomes aware of His presence. Then the book of the sacred author or the preacher to whom I am listening will disappear; God Himself speaks, and He is speaking to me. The sphere of faith is not actually abandoned, but for a moment I am raised above it to an experimental knowledge of God.

*

All theology has ultimately only the one aim to clear the way for God Himself. The Areopagite says explicitly that this is the goal of his symbolic theology. It is addressed to a select circle and wants to do more than merely instruct in the content of the faith. It is addressed to those who have already experienced a certain illumination, and hence are striving for sanctity. Symbolic theology tries to guide such persons by showing them in image a world that surpasses the senses. It would detach them increasingly from the sensible world and its desires, and lead them to a point where they will no longer need such images. Symbolic theology attempts to 'lead them by the hand' (*Celest. Hier.* 1.2), first away from the sensible to the spiritual and suprasensible world, and finally to the summit of union with the One. Theology itself cannot achieve this last step; this is reserved to God. It can only point the direction.

Experimental knowledge has been called before 'the fulfilment of faith'. This indicates that faith aims at the same state as is actually given in experimental knowledge. This is the general characteristic of 'intention' and 'fulfilment'. When I come to see with my own eyes something I had known only by hearsay, e.g. a famous work of art or a beautiful old city, that which I actually perceive as existent has already been part of my inner world before. It had reached me in a certain way through reports heard or read, and I had been touched by it. This is the meaning of fulfilment. This is even more true of faith. We regard the Scriptures as the Word of God, because He approaches us through them, revealing Himself and making known His demands. As long as I am looking at the Scriptures only in bare faith, they are but the word spoken in His name. But even this mediated word can establish contact with Him and make me feel interiorly touched. It is due to this characteristic of faith by which it transcends itself—St. Thomas calls it 'the beginning of eternal life within us'—that we can recognize God when He suddenly makes us feel His presence or even shows Himself visibly*; it also enables us to understand what others have said about their own experiences of God, though we ourselves may have had none.

The same considerations apply to a certain extent also to the natural knowledge of God. Supposing a man grew up without knowledge of the faith but were sensitive to God's traces in nature, in his own soul and in human life, he might feel his faults to be sins and consider a loss he suffered as a divine punishment. He might easily understand that God can be said to show His wrath or to be a consuming fire. Though natural knowledge of God may be very imperfect and vague, and in need of being corrected and enriched by faith, it yet points mysteriously to the goal that will be reached only in the experimental knowledge of God. In some way God is met even on the level of natural knowledge, and thus He can be 'recognized' when He actually makes Himself 'present' to such a person.

So it seems that there must be very many people capable, at least in principle, of understanding the image-language of symbolic theology. What then does it mean that this theology "hides what is holy from the desecrating eyes of the multitude"? Are there any people left incapable of understanding symbolic theo-

---

* A strange expression, perhaps referring to Isaias' vision she had discussed before. Ed.

logy? Such persons undoubtedly exist. Today no less than in the
time of Dionysius the Scriptural images are exposed to the same
crude misunderstandings as those mentioned by him. And even
if they are not misinterpreted, they may still meet with a complete
lack of understanding. There are several reasons for this.

*

As has been said before, our world points beyond itself in many
ways, thus inviting the mind to transcend its boundaries. But
these hints are not so clear that they could not be missed, nor so
unequivocal as to lead infallibly to the goal. Here as well as in
many similar situations natural disposition and upbringing will
play a decisive part. A man lacking practical sense will be incapable of seeing 'what a thing is good for' and how to use it. If he
is not well trained, he will always live in a hazy, helpless state
of mind. Some people are also lacking in 'religious sense', and
may quite possibly remain blind to the 'hints' by which the world
points to God unless this defect is remedied by a good education.
According to the doctrine of the Church the human mind *can*
know God by its natural capacities. But it is not said that everyone *will* do so in all circumstances. If St. Paul says (Rom. 1 : 20)
that the pagans are without excuse because God can be known
from creation, this must be taken as referring to the pagan world
as a whole, in which aids were certainly never lacking. Further,
the apostle considered them guilty because, despite their knowledge of God, they did not worship Him in the right way. Thus
to some the Scriptures remain a sealed book unless they are
assisted by some special grace. They stop at the immediate literal
sense and are incapable of penetrating the images. Hence they
cannot account for the 'greater dissimilarity' and develop a poor
or unworthy idea of God, or even become atheists because they
find such an idea repulsive. They may also reject not God, but
the testimony of Scripture.

It is doubtful whether such lack of faith, that is complete
ignorance of God, can exist without personal guilt, and hence
the image-language of the Bible actually be inaccessible to some.

If the latter should be the case, we can yet not deny *all* human guilt. We may here disregard original sin and the darkening of the mind it has caused. Yet no man grows up completely separated from others; and thus society would be responsible, because it failed to supply the testimony that might have opened the eyes of the person in question. In most cases, however, the unbeliever will himself also be responsible for his blindness. No one can live under conditions that would leave him quite without any testimony of God. It will be his own fault if he refuses to admit it, and even fails to make some effort to follow up the information received. If, at a later date this should result in complete inability to know, if the actual lack of recognition is replaced by an incapacity to recognize at all, then these effects will ultimately be his own doing. This is evidently even more so if there is not only actual lack of faith but definite atheism or hostility to God on principle. It is not within the scope of this article to examine the causes of such an attitude. But we must come to understand the fact that symbolic theology may in the end come to hide God rather than to reveal Him. It is easy to see that the eyes of a sincere unbeliever are unable to pierce the veil. Such a man, however, is not one of those who are not meant to see. It seems rather in accordance with the meaning of 'theology' that he should be taught to see. Some people fail to come to a knowledge of God because they are lazy and dull of mind. In such instances the inability to see may be considered a punishment. It is even more understandable that those evil minds be struck with blindness that *refuse* to believe, yet read the Scriptures in order to turn their very words into weapons against revealed truth. There is a passage indicating that Dionysius may actually have thought on such lines. In the second paragraph of his seventh letter, which is addressed to Polycarp, he answers the sophist Apollophanes who had criticized him for fighting Greek philosophy with its own tenets. Dionysius, in his turn, reproaches the Greek for trying to use divine wisdom against God. The particular instance, however, to which Dionysius refers, can hardly be interpreted as a misuse of Scripture. In any case the remark has a wider significance. It throws some light on the theological controversies of the age, when pagan and Christian writers alternately used the weapons of their respective opponents.

*

We have been trying to show that, in all true knowledge of God, God Himself comes to man, though His presence is not actually felt except when it is a case of experimental knowledge. In natural knowledge, God approaches man through images, words and various effects; in faith through His self-revelation in His Word. Whenever we are concerned with the question of knowing a person, there is not only the possibility of self-manifestation, but also of its opposite, barring the approach to knowledge, and further the possibility of hiding behind one's work. This work will then still have its real meaning and significance, but it will no longer be the means of contact between two minds. God will let Himself be found by those who seek Him. Therefore He first desires to be sought. Hence we shall understand why natural revelation is not perfectly clear and unequivocal, but rather a spur inviting further search, whereas supernatural revelation answers the questions raised by natural revelation. Faith is already finding God and means that He lets Himself be found to a certain extent, not only in the sense that He allows us to be told something about Him by His Word, but also that He actually lets Himself be found in it. Faith is a gift that must be accepted; here divine and human freedom meet. But it belongs to its nature that it must ask for more. Being a dark knowledge lacking true insight, faith arouses the desire for unveiled brightness; being an indirect meeting it makes us wish to meet God directly, the very content of faith excites this longing by promising the beatific vision. On the other hand we can also understand that God withdraws from those who fail to follow His call to seek further, who remain unmoved and spiritually indifferent to His self-revelation, or do not seek Him there, but the satisfaction of their own ends, so that they may even turn against Him. If a man will not accept God's word as the word of *God*, it will turn into a dead word. It will no longer be alive, pointing beyond itself to the sphere whence it comes, that is the kingdom of the divine Spirit. The pagans may find a confirmation of their idolatry in some of the images, the sophists discover contradictions between different passages; the educationists and moralists may be scandalized by many things, because they remain obtusely ignorant of the hidden meaning.

The 'hidden sense' may be more or less hidden. As has been pointed out before, Dionysius lumps together very different things under the term 'symbol'. He understands by this visible images of the invisible, which yet bear a true image-relation to the latter, such as the consuming fire, but also others in which this relation is not immediately obvious but may be established by thoughtful comparison and reasoned reflexion, as e.g. in the relation of the mixing bowl to divine Providence. The latter would now be called an allegory rather than a symbol. In other examples that have been mentioned the symbols have no longer a meaning that can easily be ascertained. This is the case with the parables. Jesus Himself added an explanation to His parable of the sower, because His disciples asked for it. Before, he had closed His story with the words: "He that hath ears to hear, let him hear". These words suggest that the true meaning is not to be found on the surface and will not be clear to everyone. The person who hears the parable has first to grasp its meaning, which demands an intense activity of the mind. But then he must also be aware that this whole mental complex points in a definite direction beyond itself. He must disengage from the story a 'type', in the sense of a general form, which is to serve as a directive enabling the mind to form behind the first mental complex a second one, in which the same form occurs again, but now invested with the meaning its author originally intended to convey. Even in the case of comparisons and parables invented by men, few people are capable of such intellectual discovery and reconstruction. How much less will this be the case, even with the best intention, if God Himself is the author. Not even the disciples were capable of this, though to them it was given to know the mysteries of the kingdom of heaven (Matth. 13: 11), so the Lord had to explain the hidden meaning to them. In a similar way He later taught the two disciples on the way to

Emmaus how to understand the messianic prophecies and their bearing upon His passion and glorification. Only when the Holy Ghost had been sent were the apostles able to do this exegetical work themselves.

*

We have briefly mentioned the diversity of symbolic relations to indicate that there are different degrees and ways of hiddenness, to which correspond different degrees and ways of symbolic knowledge. The most general approach is provided in the image-relation properly so called. The parables, on the other hand, offer divine truth as it were in a locked casket. In many instances men are required to look for the key, in others this is supplied in the form of an additional explanation or an inner illumination. It may also happen that a kind of 'office of the key' is conferred on individuals or groups, who have received the gift of scriptural exegesis. This point of view makes it possible to understand the Dionysian 'hierarchies'. God reveals Himself first of all to the pure spirits, whose natural capacity of understanding is greater than ours, and in whom the divine Light meets no interior obstacles. These spirits are given the office to transmit the light they receive, and this is taken over and continued in the human order by the 'ecclesiastical hierarchies', whose members are called to an 'angelic' life and service. Dionysius emphasizes on the one hand that the revelation is given us through the angels *(Celest. Hier.* 4.4*)*, on the other that Christ is the head of both hierarchies, giving each a share in the divine life according to its nature. The angels share it in a purely spiritual manner, men through the priestly office and the symbols of the liturgy *(Eccl. Hier.* 1.1ff). Thus the office of the angels as mediators recedes into the background. The highest grades of the ecclesiastical hierarchy are said to receive the 'sacred gift' from God Himself, no mention being made of the angels as mediators *(ibid.* 1.5*)*. It is their duty to receive the divine mysteries with a purified mind and to take charge of them. This also includes preaching and interpreting the Word of God. Corresponding to the various ways and degrees of hiddenness there are different ways and degrees of revelation, degrees of office and difference in the extent to which a person is forbidden or allowed approach.

*

The variety of symbols constitutes a series of degrees even within symbolic theology. This is repeated in the other 'theologies' which Dionysius distinguishes from the former. The 'spiritual names of God' (such as the Good, Being, the One) cannot be understood even in their immediate significance. Hence they appeal only to a circle of chosen minds. We need to inquire more closely into the relation these names bear to God and how He may be known through them. It seems possible to show that here it is no longer a question of the mere relation of sign or reproduction, yet still of a 'mysterious revelation'. This seems to agree also with the opinion of Dionysius himself, though he distinguishes this theology as 'manifest' from symbolic theology as 'secret'. This 'positive theology' therefore must be complemented and corrected by a 'negative theology'. In both will be found something of that which makes all knowledge about God a real knowledge of Him, namely the personal meeting with God. When this meeting finally becomes a person's actual experience, being no longer mediated by images, parables, ideas or anything else that may be named, we shall have reached the level of 'mysterious revelation' in the strict sense, that is 'mystical theology' or the self-revelation of God in silence. This is the summit to which lead the degrees of the knowledge of God.

Thus we may state once more: God Himself is the First Theologian. All speaking about God presupposes God's own speaking. His most real speaking is that before which human speech is silenced, which human words cannot comprehend nor the language of images express. It means that the man whom God addresses is seized by Him and asked to surrender himself in order to hear it. Such rapture is usually associated with his vocation as a 'theologian'. God wants to speak to the people who stay in the plain through those to whom He speaks on the summit of the mountain. Therefore He deigns to speak to them and through them, but also without their mediation, in human words and in images that men can understand. He gives to His theologians the words and images by which they can present Him to others. To these latter He Himself speaks as a 'symbolic theologian', through nature, through man's inner experiences, and through His vestiges in human life and in the history of the world, thus rendering people capable of understanding the language of the theologians.

*

We have been discussing a set of problems, surveying the ground they cover with a minimum of theological presuppositions. A further elucidation of the concept of God as the 'First Theologian' in theological terms would have to start from the most authentic example of God's speaking in the Divine Word Himself. The Word made Flesh would then have to be considered as the first symbol.

B. SCIENCE OF THE CROSS
The Night

Detachment is described as a night through which the soul has to pass. It is this in a threefold sense: in regard to the point of departure, the way and the goal. The starting point is the desire for the things of this world which the soul must renounce. But this renunciation places it as it were in darkness and nothingness. Hence it is called night. The world we perceive with our senses is naturally the firm ground that carries us, the house where we feel at home, that feeds us, provides for all our needs, and is the source of our joys and pleasures. If it is taken away from us, or if we are compelled to withdraw from it, it is truly as if the ground were cut away from under our feet, and all around us were night, as if we ourselves had to drown and vanish. But this is not so. In fact we are placed in a safe way, though it is dark and shrouded in night: the way of faith. It is a way, for it leads to the goal of union. But it is a nocturnal way, for compared with the clear insight of natural reason faith is a dark knowledge: it makes us acquainted with something, but we cannot see it. Hence it must be said that the goal, too, which we attain by the way of faith is night: on earth God remains hidden for us even in the blissful union. Our spiritual eye is not adapted to His too radiant light and looks as if into the darkness of night. But just as the cosmic night is not equally dark throughout, so the mystical night, too, has its periods and corresponding degrees. The drowning of the world of sense is like the beginning of the night, which still leaves us the dusk of daylight. Faith, on the other hand, is midnight darkness, because here not only sense activity is eliminated, but also the natural knowledge of reason. But when the soul finds God, it is as if the dawn of the new day of eternity were already breaking into its night.

Freedom

Every human being is free, and is confronted with decisions

97

every day and hour. Now the inmost part of the soul is the place where God dwells 'all alone', as long as the soul has not attained to the perfect union of love; and our holy Mother Teresa calls this the seventh mansion, which opens to the soul only in the mystical marriage. This raises the question whether the soul can decide in perfect freedom only when it has reached the highest stage of perfection. Here we have to take into account that the soul's own activity evidently decreases, the more it approaches this inmost sphere. And when it has reached it, God will work everything in it, itself will have nothing more to do than to receive. Yet its share of freedom is expressed in just this receiving. But beyond this, freedom is involved in a much more decisive way: God here works everything only because the soul surrenders itself to Him perfectly. And this surrender is itself the highest achievement of its freedom.

EDUCATIONAL WRITINGS

A. THE VOCATION OF MAN AND WOMAN ACCORDING TO NATURE AND TO GRACE

In ordinary usage the term 'vocation' or 'calling' *(Beruf)** has come to be watered down, so that little is preserved of its original meaning. When children leave school we consider which calling or profession they are to take up; and people have debated for a long time whether women should enter any of them or remain in the house. When used in this sense the word usually means no more than a kind of paid occupation. Only in certain contexts does it preserve its original meaning, for example if one says that a person has missed his vocation, or in speaking of a religious vocation. In such phrases we express that a vocation or calling is something to which a man is called.

Now what does this mean: to be called? There must have been a call made by someone to somebody else for a certain thing, and in a comprehensible way. We say, for example, that a scholar has been called to a professor's chair. The call then comes from an institution such as a university or a faculty; it is made to a man whom natural talent and education seem to call to the activity to which he is actually being called, that is to work as a scholar and teacher. The call comes to him in the form of a request made in set traditional phrases. I have just been using a strange expression: he is called to what he seems to be called. Hence the call by a human institution evidently presupposes another call which those people believe they recognize, and which they express: i.e. he is called by natural talent and education. He himself and many others have contributed to the latter both voluntarily and involuntarily; but it developed on the foundation of his talent in the most comprehensive sense of the term, including all the gifts he has brought to his life. Now a man's vocation, i.e. the work which he is destined to accomplish, is indicated by his nature. It

---

* The German term *Beruf* is the exact equivalent of profession, but is derived from *rufen*, call. The English terms calling or vocation preserve actually much more of the religious meaning than the German, therefore I have translated *Beruf* by any of the three possible English equivalents, according to the context. Ed.

will mature and become obvious to others in the course of his life, so that they can speak of his 'vocation' in the happy case that he has found 'his place' in life. But a man's nature and the course of his life are no gifts or whims of chance, but, seen with the eyes of faith, they are the work of God. And thus God Himself is ultimately the one who calls. He calls every man to something to which all are called, and every individual to something to which he is called personally; moreover, He calls men and women as such to particular ends, as our subject presupposes. It does not seem easy to recognize to what man and woman are called, because it has for so long been a very controversial subject. Yet there are a number of ways in which the call comes to us: God Himself tells us about it in the words of the Old and the New Testaments. It is also inscribed in the very nature of man and woman; history enlightens us on it, and finally the demands of our time speak their own language emphatically. Thus we are faced with a web of manifold threads, but we do not think the pattern so confused that it should not be possible, by calmly examining it, to trace some clear lines. Thus we will dare to approach the question of the vocation of man and woman.

The first words of Holy Scripture that treat of man assign a common vocation to both: "Let us make man to our image and likeness; and let him have dominion over the fishes of the sea and the fowls of the air, and the beasts, and the whole earth, and every creeping creature that moveth upon the earth. And God created man to his own image; to the image of God he created him. Male and female he created them. And God blessed them, saying: Increase and multiply, and fill the earth, and subdue it, and rule over the fishes of the sea, and the fowls of the air, and all living creatures that move upon the earth". (Gen. 1: 26-28).

Thus the differentiation into man and woman is mentioned at once in the first account of the creation of man. Both together are given a threefold task: they are to be the image of God, to produce posterity, and to rule the earth. Nothing is said here about this threefold vocation being carried out by each of them in a different way; it could at most be inferred from the mention of the difference of sex.

The second passage which deals at greater length with the creation of man tells us a little more about the relation between the sexes. (Gen. 2 : 7ff.). It describes the creation of Adam, how he was placed in the 'paradise of pleasure' to inhabit and cultivate it, and how the animals were brought to him so that he should give them names. "But for Adam there was not found a helper like himself". The Hebrew expression here is almost untranslatable: *"Eser kenegdo"*, quite literally: "A help as it were opposite him". One might think of a mirror in which man could see his own nature. This is the view of those translators who speak of "a helper like himself". But it can also be taken to mean a counterpart, so that both are indeed like each other, but not altogether equal, but complementing each other as the two hands of a man. "And the Lord God said: It is not good for man to be alone; let us make him a help like unto himself". And God caused Adam to fall asleep and took one of his ribs, built up a woman and led her to Adam. "And Adam said: This now is bone of my bones, and flesh of my flesh; she shall be called woman, because she was taken out of man. Wherefore a man shall leave father and mother, and shall cleave to his wife; and they shall be two in one flesh. And they were both naked, to wit Adam and his wife, and were not ashamed". (Gen. 2 : 23-25). The fact that man was created first indicates a certain superiority. Why it would not have been good for him to be alone is again inferred from the word of God. God created man in His own image. Now God is one in three: as the Son is generated from the Father, and the Spirit proceeds from the Father and the Son, so analogically woman originates from man, and posterity from both. And again, God is love; but love cannot be between less than two, as Pope St. Gregory says in his homily on the sending of the disciples two by two.

There is no question here of a dominion of man over woman. She is called his companion and help, and man is told that he will cleave to her and that they will both be one flesh. This indicates that the life of the first human couple is to be considered as the most intimate union of love, that they worked together in complete harmony as if they were one single being, just as before the fall the faculties in each of them were in perfect harmony. Senses and spirit were in full accord with each other without the possibility of opposition. Hence they did not desire each other inordinately. This is expressed by the words: "And they were both naked . . . and were not ashamed".

After the fall God's call to men and men's calling appear essentially changed. Eve had let herself be enticed by the tempter and in her turn tempted man to sin. Adam is first called to account. He places the guilt on the woman: "The woman whom thou gavest me to be my companion, gave me of the tree, and I did eat". (Gen. 3: 12). This sounds also as if he were accusing God. Now judgement is pronounced first on the serpent and on the woman; then on Adam himself. His excuse has not been accepted: "Because thou hast hearkened to the voice of thy wife, and hast eaten of the tree, whereof I commanded thee that thou shouldst not eat, cursed is the earth in thy work; with labour and toil shalt thou eat thereof all the days of thy life. Thorns and thistles shall it bring forth to thee; and thou shalt eat the herbs of the earth. In the sweat of thy face shalt thou eat bread till thou return to the earth, out of which thou wast taken: for dust thou art, and into dust thou shalt return". (Gen. 3: 17-19). Disobedience is punished by the loss of his undisputed dominion over the earth and of the willing service of the lower creatures. From now on he will have to fight against them in the painful struggle for his daily bread, working hard for miserable results.

The woman is punished in a different way: "I will multiply thy sorrows, and thy conceptions. In sorrow shalt thou bring forth children, and thou shalt be under thy husband's power, and he shall have dominion over thee". (Gen. 3: 16). We do not know in what way the blessing of fertility would have been realized before man's fall. Its consequence is the labour of birth for the woman, and the labour of the struggle for existence for the man. In the case of the woman there is the added punishment of being subjected to man. His attempt to shift the responsibility for his sin to his wife shows that he will not be a good master. The unclouded communion of love has been destroyed. Something else has been roused instead, which they did not know before: they realized that they were naked, and they were ashamed. They themselves tried to cover their nakedness, and God provided for it. "And the Lord God made for Adam and his wife garments of skins, and clothed them". (Gen. 3:21). Lust has been roused in them, and they have to be protected against it.

Thus the relationship between man and the earth, posterity and each other has been changed. All this is the result of man's changed relation to God. The account of the creation and fall of man is full of mysteries which we shall not be able to solve. But it should not be presumptuous to formulate some questions that arise and to attempt an interpretation. Why was it forbidden to eat of the Tree of Knowledge? What kind of fruit was eaten by the woman and given to the man? And why did the tempter approach the woman first? Obviously man was not without knowledge before the fall. For he had been created after the image of God, had given names to all living beings, and was called to rule the earth. On the contrary, he is endowed with a far more perfect knowledge than after the fall. Hence it must have been a quite particular knowledge with which we are here concerned. The serpent actually speaks of a knowledge of good and evil. Now we cannot possibly assume that men before the fall would have been without knowledge of the good. They had a more perfect knowledge of God, that is of the highest good, and hence of any particular good. But they were probably destined to be preserved from the knowledge of evil which one gains by doing it. The immediate consequence of the first sin gives an indication in what it may have consisted; for it results in the fact that man and woman were now looking at each other in a different way; they had lost the innocence of their intercourse with each other. Thus the first sin may not have consisted only purely formally in disobedience to God; but the forbidden thing which the serpent presented as desirable to the woman, and she in her turn to the man, will have been something definite, namely a mode of union contradicting the original order.* The

* This is a private speculation of the author not supported by the majority of Catholic theologians, who hold that the first sin was a sin of pride, and that the propagation of the human race before the fall would have taken place in the same way as now, but unaccompanied by unruly passion or 'concupiscence.' Ed

fact that the tempter first approached woman with this suggestion may indicate that she was more easily accessible, not because she was generally more easily moved to evil (both being still free from an inclination to evil) but because what was proposed was more important to her. It is to be assumed that from the first her life was to be more powerfully affected by all that concerned the procreation and education of posterity. The difference in punishment for man and woman points to the same. According to the wording of the Biblical account the loss of eternal life seems to be included in the expulsion from paradise; the Lord pronounces the sentence of death, with which Adam had been threatened from the beginning as the punishment of disobedience. But before he is expelled, he is given a promise, contained in the words that announce the punishment of the serpent. "I will put enmities between thee and the woman, and thy seed and her seed: she shall crush thy head, and thou shalt lie in wait for her heel". (Gen. 3: 15). This passage is generally interpreted as referring to the Mother of God and to our Lord. But this does not exclude the other meaning, that even the first woman, to whom Adam gave the name of Mother of all the living, and all her successors have been set as their special task to fight against evil and thus to prepare the restoration of life. When her first child was born, Eve said: "God has given me a son". This seems to indicate that she sensed a blessing given her in her son. And later the women of Israel saw their vocation in bringing forth descendants who were to see the day of salvation.

Thus a peculiar connexion has been established between fall and redemption, and the facts connected with both these events are strangely similar. As temptation first came to a woman, so God's message of grace also was first announced to a woman, and in both cases the Yes pronounced by a woman decided the fate of all mankind. At the beginning of the new kingdom of God we see not a human couple like the first, but Mother and Son. The Son of God is son of man through His Mother, but not through a human father. The Son of God chose not the ordinary way of human procreation in order to become man. Does this not seem to indicate that from the first sin a stain attached to this way, which could only be removed by the kingdom of grace? And does it not also indicate the nobility of motherhood as the purest and highest union of human beings?* It is the privilege of the female sex that a woman was allowed to help found the new kingdom of God; it is the privilege of the male sex that mankind was redeemed by the *Son* of man, the new Adam. This again expressed man's superior position.

The Lord has unequivocally affirmed that the new kingdom of God would reform the relations between the sexes, i.e. it would abolish the state of affairs brought about by the fall and restore the original order (Matth. 19: 1-12; Mark 10: 1-12). In answer to the question of a Pharisee whether a man is allowed to divorce his wife Jesus answered: "Moses by reason of the hardness of your heart permitted you to put away your wives; but from the beginning it was not so". He refers to the passage in the creation account: They shall be two in one flesh; and promulgates the commandment of the new law: "What therefore God hath joined together, let no man put asunder". But besides, He establishes as something entirely new the ideal of virginity, such as it put before us by the example of the Virgin-Mother and of the Lord Himself.**

The relationship between man and woman is most fully argued in the letters of St. Paul. The much discussed passage of 1 Corinthians 11: 3ff runs as follows: "But I would have you know that the head of every man is Christ: and the head of the woman is the man: and the head of Christ is God. Every man praying or prophesying with his head covered disgraceth his head. But every woman praying or prophesying with her head not covered disgraceth her head: for it is all one as if she were shaven . . . The man indeed ought not to cover his head: because his is the image and glory of God. But the woman is the glory of the man. For the man is not of the woman: but the woman of the man. For the man was not created for the woman: but the woman for the man . . . Yet neither is the man without the woman, nor the woman without the man, in the Lord". We do not think we

* See preceding note.
** According to the teaching of the majority of Catholic theologians the ideal of virginity would have been unnecessary if man had not fallen. Ed.

shall offend the apostle if we say that in this instruction to the Corinthians divine and human, temporal and eternal things are mixed up. Hair styles and clothes are matters of custom, as St. Paul says himself at the end of this passage: "But if any man seem to be contentious, we have no such custom, nor the Church of God". (ibid. 11 : 16). If his decision on the appearance of the Corinthian woman in church was binding for the Church he had founded, this does not mean that it should be valid for all times. What he says about the fundamental relationship between man and woman must be judged in a different light, for it claims to be an interpretation of the divine order of creation and redemption, man and woman are destined to lead together *one* life as if they were a single being. To the man, as to the one who was created first, is due the direction in this community of life. Yet one has the impression that the interpretation does not reproduce the original and the redemptive orders in their integrity. In stressing the relationship of subjection and even more in assuming a mediatorship of man between the Redeemer and woman he is still influenced by the order of fallen nature. Neither the account of the creation nor the Gospel knows such a mediatorship in the relation of woman with God. On the other hand, it is known both to the Mosaic and to Roman law. The apostle himself, however, knows another order, since he says in the same letter to the Corinthians, when writing about marriage and virginity: "The unbelieving husband is sanctified by the believing wife", and "How knowest thou, wife, whether thou shalt save thy husband?" This is the order of the Gospel, according to which every soul is gained for the supernatural life by Christ, and everyone who is sanctified by union with Christ, whether man or woman, is called to be a mediator.

The relationship between man and woman is treated even more explicitly in the Letter to the Ephesians: "Let women be subject to their husbands, as to the Lord: Because the husband is the head of the wife, as Christ is the head of the church. He is the saviour of his body. Therefore as the church is subject to Christ: so also let the wives be to their husbands in all things. Husbands, love your wives, as Christ also loved the church and delivered himself up for it: that he might sanctify it, cleansing it by the laver of water in the word of life: That he might present it to himself, a glorious church, not having spot or wrinkle or any such thing; but that it should be holy and without blemish. So also ought men to love their wives as their own bodies. He that loveth his wife loveth himself. For no man ever hated his own flesh, but nourisheth and cherisheth it, as also Christ doth the church: Because we are members of his body, of his flesh and of his bones. For this cause shall a man leave his father and mother: and shall cleave to his wife. And they shall be two in one flesh. This is a great sacrament: but I speak in Christ and in the church. Nevertheless, let every one of you in particular love his wife as himself: and let the wife fear her husband". (Eph. 5: 22-33).

This passage outlines the matrimonial relationship between Christians. The Lord Himself, referring to the words of Genesis, has emphasized only its indissolubility and the unity of the two in the one flesh, whereas here it is explained in detail how this unity is to be conceived. Just as in the individual organism all the members are directed by the head, and thus the harmony is preserved, so also the greater organism must have a head, and if the organism is sound there can be no question as to which is the head and which are the members, and what are their respective functions. It should not be forgotten that we are here concerned with a symbolic relationship. The parable of Christ and the Church reminds us of this. Christ is our head, and His divine life flows into us His members, if we belong to Him in love and are subject to Him in obedience. The Godman, who is the head, has His independent existence outside this mystical Body. The members also have their independent being as free and reasonable creatures, and the mystical Body is built up through the love of the Head and the free submission of the members. Each member of the mystical Body has its function according to the talents given to him. They are qualities both of mind and body, and the Head in His wisdom uses the members according to their gifts. Through the divine power of the Head each member has been endowed with talents that can be used for the profit of the whole Body. It is the end of this whole organism which is the mystical Body of Christ, that each member, being a whole man consisting of body and soul, should attain to the fullness of salvation as a child of God and glorify in his own way the whole Body, the communion of saints. If the man is to be the head of the woman—and we may logically add of the whole family—in the same sense as Christ is the head of the Church, it will be his task so to direct this small image of the great mystical Body that each of its members by fully developing his gifts may contribute to the well-being of the whole and itself attain to salvation. The husband is not actually Christ; he has not the power to bestow gifts. But he is able to develop (or to retard) the gifts that are there, in the way in which men can help each other to develop their gifts. It will be his wisdom not to let these atrophy, but to cause them to unfold and grow for the good of the whole. And since he himself is not perfect like Christ, but a creature with certain gifts and many weaknesses, it may be his highest wisdom to let his weaknesses be compensated by the gifts of a complementary member, just as it may be the highest political wisdom of the sovereign to let his better qualified ministers do the governing. It is, however, essential for the organism that this should be done under the direction of the head. If the body rebels against the head, the organism will flourish as little as if the head lets the body atrophy.

While the Letter to the Ephesians deals with the married life, the apostle discusses the position of women in the congregation even more explicitly in the First Letter to Timothy. "In like manner, women also in decent apparel: adorning themselves with modesty and sobriety, not with plaited hair, or gold, or pearls, or costly attire: But, as it becometh women professing godliness, with good works. Let the woman learn in silence with all subjection. But I suffer not a woman to teach, nor to use authority over the man: but to be in silence. For Adam was first formed: then Eve. And Adam was not seduced but the woman, being seduced, was in the transgression. Yet she shall be saved through child-bearing: if she continue in faith and love and sanctification with sobriety". (1 Tim. 2:9-15).

Here we feel even more strongly than in the Letter to the Corinthians that the original and the redemptive orders are submerged in the order of fallen nature, and that the apostle still speaks as the Jew who is guided by the spirit of the Law. The evangelical conception of virginity seems entirely forgotten. What is said here, and may have been suitable in view of certain abuses in the Greek Churches, is not to be considered as of obligation for the fundamental teaching on the relationship between the sexes. It is too much opposed to the words and practice of our Lord, who had women among His most intimate friends and proved everywhere in His redemptive work that the soul of woman was as much His concern as the soul of man.* It also contradicts the words of St. Paul himself, which express the spirit of the Gospel most purely: "Wherefore the Law was our pedagogue in Christ: that we might be justified by faith. But after the faith is come, we are no longer under the pedagogue . . . There is neither Jew nor Greek; there is neither bond nor free: there is neither male nor female. For you are all one in Christ Jesus". (Gal. 3:28). Before going on to interpret the Scriptural data by the nature of man and woman such as it is accessible to our knowledge, we would summarize the results that have already been acquired.

The vocation of man and woman is not quite the same in the original order, the order of fallen nature and the order of redemption. Originally they were both required to preserve their own similarity to God, their dominion over the earth and the preservation of the race. The superiority of man that seems implied in the fact that he was created first is not yet explained in detail. After their fall their relationship is changed from a pure communion of love to one of governing and subordination tainted by lust. The hard struggle for existence has been assigned primarily to man, the labour of birth to woman. But there is a promise of redemption, because woman is to fight evil, and the male sex will be exalted in the Son of Man who is to come. The Redemption will restore the original order. The superiority of

* Here the author's feminist tendencies have evidently carried her too far in her criticism of the Apostle and allowed her to forget that his words are inspired. Ed.

man is revealed in the fact that the Saviour came into the world as man. The feminine sex is honoured in that He was born of a human mother. A woman becomes the gate through which God entered into the human race. Adam was the human type that pointed to the future divine-human king of creation, hence in the kingdom of God every man is to reproduce Christ, and in the community of marriage the loving care of Christ for the Church. The woman, being freely and lovingly subject to her husband, is to honour the image of Christ in him and to be herself the image of the Mother of God; and this also means being herself an image of Christ.

If we attempt to describe the nature of man and woman on the basis of natural knowledge, we shall receive a vivid interpretation of what the Word of God has suggested to us. On the other hand, this latter will be a guide by which to interpret the evidence of life. We shall find in it again the traces of the original order of creation, of the fall and of the redemption.

Man's body and mind are equipped for fight and conquest, in accordance with his original vocation to subject the world and be its king and master. Thus there is a threefold urge in him: he wants to subdue it by knowledge and thus to make it his own, but also to possess it with all the enjoyments it offers, and lastly to make it his own creation by forming it. It is due to the limitation of human nature, which it shares with every created thing, but even more to the deterioration of all his powers in the state of original sin, that man is unable to achieve in equal measure all that is implied in his dominion over the earth. If the desire for knowledge is strong in him and he uses all his energy to satisfy it, he will to a great extent be forced to renounce the possession and enjoyment of the good things of life as well as creative work. If he pursues riches and pleasure, he will hardly achieve pure (i.e. devoid of personal interests) knowledge and creative work. But if he is wholly intent on making a small world of his own creation, whether as a farmer, an artist or a politician etc., pure knowledge and the enjoyment of the good things of life will have to take the second place. And in each of these spheres the single achievement will be the more perfect, the more restricted the field of activity. Thus just the desire to produce as perfect a work as possible will lead to onesidedness and cause the other talents to atrophy.

Yet, for fallen nature the onesided effort can also easily become a perverted effort. Knowledge will not reverently stop at the barriers imposed on it, but will try to break them by violence. Moreover, knowledge itself may bar its own way to what is not on principle inaccessible to it, by refusing to bow to the law of things; instead it seeks to possess them arbitrarily, or lets its judgement be clouded by desires and lusts. The perversion of man's dominion has similar results with regard to the good things of the earth. Instead of reverently and joyfully preserving and developing created things, he greedily exploits them even unto destruction, or senselessly piles them up without being able to use them properly and to enjoy what he has acquired. Related to this is the perversion of creative work that violently distorts and destroys natural things and invents and creates grotesque caricatures.

This change of kingship into brutal tyranny shows itself also in man's relation to woman. According to the original order she was given him as a companion and helpmate. Hence she is equipped in the same way as he in order to assist him in dominating the earth: she, too, is capable of knowledge, enjoyment and creative work. But normally in her these gifts are less intense; thus, on the other hand, she is less in danger of being completely immersed in one of them to the detriment of the others. This indicates a form of co-operation in which the woman could develop her gifts by the side of man in their common tasks, while he would be preserved from becoming inordinately onesided by the more harmonious development of her gifts. But in the state of punishment after the fall this companionship was changed into a state of domination which is often brutally enforced. The natural gifts of a woman and their best possible development are irrelevant, and she is exploited as a means to an end in the service of a work or for the satisfaction of a man's desire. So it may easily come about that the tyrant becomes the slave of lust, and thus the slave of the slave who is to satisfy it.

The perversion of the relations between man and woman is connected with that of the attitude towards posterity. Procreation was originally meant to be the task of both. Since, owing to their differences, both depend on completing each other, this dependence is even more emphasized in their relationship to their children. On the one hand the undeveloped nature of the child makes it necessary to nurse and protect it and to guide its growth. Owing to the close physical relationship between mother and child and woman's special capacity for sharing and devoting herself to another's life, she will have the principal part in its education, which will also be helped by her stronger instinct for the harmonious development of human talents. On the other hand, the demands of motherhood make it imperative that man should protect and care for mother and child. Moreover, because he is more energetic and gifted for outstanding achievements, he has also a duty to instruct. And finally, because he is king of all creation, he has also to care for the noblest of all earthly creatures. Moreover, we have to consider also that not only man and woman have been created to complement each other, but also the generations that follow one another. For each subsequent generation is called to achieve something new of its own, and it is one of the essential tasks of education to observe reverently the new things that want to grow in the young generation. Thus fatherhood appears to be an original vocation of man, given to him beside his particular calling. The vocation of the father may be abused in many ways. On the one hand he may shun his duties, in the lowest form by abusing sexual intercourse for the mere satisfaction of his instincts, without giving any thought to his descendants, perhaps even at their cost. On a higher level he may indeed shoulder his material responsibilities, but neglect his share in their education. On the other hand there is the danger that a father will perform his duties brutally, restricting the mother's responsibilities to the merely physical sphere and depriving her of her higher tasks, while he himself violently represses all the legitimate aspirations of the new generation.

All weaknesses in man's nature that cause him to miss his original vocation are rooted in the perversion of his relation to

THE VOCATION OF MAN AND WOMAN

God. He can only fulfil his principal task of being the image of God, if he seeks to develop his powers in humble submission to His guidance. He must seek knowledge in the form and within the limits sanctioned by God; he must enjoy God's creatures reverently and gratefully for His glory; he must do creative work in order to complete creation in the way God has assigned to man's free action. This would mean truly to be a finite image of the divine wisdom, goodness and power. If man says to God "I will not serve", his relation to all other creatures will be perverted. We have the exact parallel in the nature of woman. According to the original order her place is by the side of man to subdue the earth and bring up posterity. But her body and soul are less suited for fight and conquest, but rather for nursing, protecting and preserving. Of the threefold attitude to the world that consists in knowing, enjoying and creatively shaping, the second is usually best suited to her. She seems more capable than man of reverently enjoying creatures. (We would remark in passing that reverent enjoyment presupposes a specific knowledge of the good things that are enjoyed, which is different from rational knowledge, but is a peculiar spiritual function that is evidently a particular feminine gift). This is evidently connected with her function of preserving and fostering posterity. It is a sense of the importance of the organic whole, of specific values and of individuals. This renders her sensitive and clear sighted for whatever wants to grow and develop and requires individual understanding. This sense of what is organic benefits not only her posterity but all other creatures, especially the opposite sex; it makes her an understanding companion and help in the enterprises of another. Hence, according to the original order of nature, man and woman evidently complement each other in this way: man's vocation is primarily to govern; his fatherhood is not subordinated to or co-ordinated with this, but included in it; whereas woman is primarily called to be a mother, her share in the government of the world being in some way implied in that.

Just as a woman's knowledge, enjoyment and action do not differ in principle from those of a man, the same forms of perversion appear in both. They are rooted in the desire to gain possession of things by violence and thus to spoil or even destroy them. The three functions just mentioned differ in importance and in the place they occupy in the whole personality and life of man and woman, hence the fall has brought about also different perversions in them. It has already been mentioned that women become one-sided and stunted in their personality less easily than men. On the other hand, the kind of onesidedness to which they are exposed is particularly dangerous. Since women are less gifted for abstract thought and creative action than for the possession and enjoyment of good things, there is the danger that they may become completely absorbed in these. If now the reverent joy in things is perverted into greed, a woman will on the one hand anxiously collect and preserve useless things, on the other sink into a life of sloth and self-indulgence. This in its turn will tend to corrupt her relationship with man. If their free companionship is threatened by his tendency to brutal despotism, she will become even more his slave by surrendering herself to her own instincts. On the other hand, her anxiety to preserve her property may also lead to a domineering attitude towards man. Her relation to her children shows similar characteristics. If a woman leads a merely sensual life she will seek to escape the duties of motherhood as much as the man those of fatherhood, unless she is preserved from this by an instinctive desire for children and an equally instinctive attachment. If a woman anxiously seeks to retain her children as if they were her property, she will try in every way to tie them to herself (also by curtailing as far as possible the rights of their father), and thus prevent their free development. By refusing to serve her husband, her children and all creatures in loving reverence, and so to further their natural development for God's honour and their natural happiness, she will prevent development and destroy happiness.

Again the root of the evil is the perversion of her relation to God. In the fall woman rebelled against God and exalted herself above man by corrupting him, therefore she was punished by being subjected to him. Because the sin to which she tempted him was very probably one of sensuality, woman is exposed more than man to the danger of succumbing entirely to a merely sensual life. And whenever this happens, she becomes once more the temptress, whereas she has expressly been commanded to fight against evil.

We have thus indicated how nature, and hence the original vocation of man and woman, can be realized: this is possible only if both once more become children of God. The redemptive work of Christ assures our adoption if we ourselves do what is in our power. The Israelites of the Old Covenant did what they were asked to do by faithfully following the Law and awaiting the Messias. For women this meant that they were humbly to be subject to men, to preserve their purity and to discipline their sensuality more strictly than men. They were to long for children in order to see in them God's salvation, and to bring them up faithfully in the fear of the Lord. Man, on the other hand, had to carry out the prescribed services of prayer and sacrifice, he had to obey the moral and social commandments, look after the well-being of his family and honour his wife as the mother of his children.

In the New Covenant man takes part in the work of redemption by the most intimate personal union with Christ; he clings to Him by faith, because He is the way of salvation who has revealed the truth and offered the means to attain beatitude; by hope which confidently expects the life promised by Him; and by love which seeks to approach Him. This love will try to know Him ever more clearly; it will contemplate His life and meditate His words and want to be united to Him most intimately in the holy Eucharist. It will share His mystical life by following the Church's Year and its liturgy. This way of salvation is the same for both sexes; it redeems both, as well as their mutual relationship.

Redemption did not restore fallen nature to its original purity by one stroke. Christ has placed salvation into the soil of mankind like a seed that must grow with the inner and outer growth of the Church and in every individual soul. Being 'on the way' like pilgrims bound for the heavenly Jerusalem, we experience in ourselves the fight of corrupt nature with the germ of grace that wants to grow in us and strives and is able to expel whatever is unhealthy. All around us we see the fruits of original sin in its most frightening forms, especially in the relationship of the sexes. Every trace of their high vocation seems to be lost in a life of unfettered licentiousness; the sexes are fighting each other for their rights, deaf to the voice of nature and of God. Yet we also see that things can be different where grace is efficacious. In Christian marriage man sees his task of being the head of his small community in his duty to ensure as well as he can their material well-being and progress; he will contribute his share so that each member may become the best that nature and grace can make it. This means that he will at times have to come forward and give a lead, at others to remain in the background, or again to intervene and oppose. If inclinations and talents stir spontaneously in his wife and children, he will allow them to develop and give them all the help he can. If he has to do with weaker natures and gifts, if he notices a lack in courage and self-confidence, he will try to bring out the hidden talents. It is one of his duties to develop the intellectual and spiritual side in his wife, and not to let her be immersed in a mere life of the instincts. He may do this by permitting her to share in his own work, or by encouraging obvious tendencies to independent activity. If he takes both possibilities away from her, seeking to confine her to a circle that is too narrow for her gifts, or even only to a life of the instincts, he will have a large share in the consequences that will result from this. He will be responsible for the fact that her higher life will atrophy, for pathological disturbances and her tendency to become too strongly attached to her husband and children, which will be a burden to them, and, moreover, for the dreariness of her life once she is left to face it alone. The same holds good for her relation to her children. On the other hand it belongs to his duties as master of the house to look after the order and harmony of family life. It is part of this duty to exhort each member not only to look after the development of his own personality, but according to his position in the household, to practise consideration to others and the self-denial that his duties entail. And, finally, his concern for the well-ordered natural life of the individuals and the family should not lead him to neglect their supernatural life. A man is meant to imitate Christ as the Head of the Church in his own small circle. Therefore he should regard it as his highest duty to set them an example in following Christ and to further, to the best of his ability, the life of grace that is stirring in them. This he will achieve the better the more closely he himself is united to the Lord.

The domestic burden which these demands place on a man in addition to his professional duties outside his home would be too heavy for him if he were not assisted by the companion who is called to shoulder more than half of it. She wants not only to develop her own personality without hindrance, but desires the same for those around her. Thus her husband will find in her his best adviser not merely for the guidance of herself and their children, but also for his own life. Indeed, he will often be best able to fulfil his duties in this respect if he lets her do things in her own way and submits to her leadership. Care for the order and beauty of the whole household is also among the natural feminine duties, since all need a harmonious atmosphere for their proper development. The feminine nature is particularly receptive to what is morally good and loathes everything that is mean and vulgar. It is thus protected against the danger of temptation and of being submerged in a wholly sensual life; this is in harmony with the mysterious prophecy of a victorious fight of the woman against the serpent, which was fulfilled by the victory which the queen of all women had won on behalf of all mankind.

Closely connected with this is the feminine receptivity to divine things. A woman desires to be personally united to the Lord and to be wholly filled and guided by His love. In a rightly ordered family life, therefore, the moral and religious education will mostly be the task of the woman. If her life is completely anchored in the life of Jesus, this will be her best protection against the danger of losing the right measure in her love for her family and her surroundings; she will not cut the ground from under her feet, on which she has to stand to be a support for others. Independent objective interests of her own would in the natural sphere counterbalance this dangerous tendency to lose herself in another's life; but these alone would lead to the opposite danger of her being unfaithful to her feminine vocation. Only if she entrusts herself wholly to the guidance of the Lord will she be sure to be led safely between Scylla and Charybdis. For whatever is given to Him is not lost, but will be preserved, purified, elevated and given the right measure.

These last suggestions lead to the question of a non-domestic profession and to the relationship of man and woman in the professional life. In view of the events of the last decades we may regard as closed that period of history which assigned to women only domestic duties, and to men the struggle of existence outside the home. Today it is not too difficult for us to see how this development could actually come about. The scientific and technical achievements which progressively replaced human labour by the work of the machine relieved women of many burdens, so that they desired to use the energies that had been released in other spheres. In the transition period much energy has been unreasonably wasted in useless trifles, and much valuable human talent has thus been frittered away. The efforts to bring about the necessary changes could not be successful without grave crises of development. On the one hand these were caused by the partisan passion of both pioneers of feminism and its opponents, either side fighting with arguments that lacked objectivity. On the other hand the crises were due to the inertia of the masses which will always cling to ancestral habits without examining their credentials. Eventually the (German) revolution (1918) brought about a sudden reversal also in this sphere, and the economic depression forced even those to take up a job who had until then given no thought to a professional training. Thus the present state is not the result of a normal development, hence not a suitable point of departure for considerations of principle.

In connexion with our former discussions we shall first have to ask whether women's professional activities outside the home are opposed to the orders of nature and grace as such. I think the answer is No. It seems to me that the original order provided for a common activity of man and woman in all spheres, though the parts would have been assigned slightly differently. The fact that the original order was changed after the fall does not mean that it was completely abolished, just as the human nature had not become wholly depraved, but preserved its original powers, though they were weakened and liable to error. All man's powers exist also in the feminine nature, even though they normally appear differently apportioned. This is surely a sign that they would be used in an occupation suited to them. It is only reasonable and in accordance with nature to transcend the circle of domestic duties where this is too narrow to allow of a full development of one's gifts. The limit beyond which we may not go, however, seems to me to be reached if the professional activities endanger the domestic life, that is the educational community of parents and children. Even in the case of man I think the divine order is violated if his professional work absorbs him to such a degree that he is completely cut off from his family life. This will be even more so in the case of a woman. Therefore we must consider as unhealthy a state of affairs in which married women are normally forced to take up work outside the home which makes it impossible for them to attend to their domestic duties. In a time when the average woman would marry and be wholly absorbed by her household duties it could be considered normal that she should be restricted to the domestic sphere.

Owing to the fall the destiny of woman has changed. First, her powers were largely restricted by the difficulties of providing even for the most primitive needs of life. In this respect the technical developments have brought a change for the better. Secondly, she was subjected to man, the scope and kind of her activities were made dependent on his will; but this was not necessarily in accordance with reason, because his intelligence and will are not infallible. Moreover, the harmony between the sexes being disturbed by the fall and both male and female natures corrupted, the subjection necessarily became the occasion for a struggle to be given opportunities for action.

The redemptive order restored the original state of things. The more it is realized in human beings, the more harmoniously will the sexes work together also in regulating their professional life. Moreover, the redemptive order brings about a fundamental change in the position of women by setting up the ideal of virginity. This breaks with the Old Testament principle that a woman can work out her salvation only by bringing forth children. Indeed, even in the Old Dispensation this principle has been set aside in the case of certain individuals called to extraordinary deeds for the people of God, such as Deborah and Judith. Now this is made into a normal way, so that women may consecrate themselves to God alone and engage in manifold activities in His service. The same St. Paul in whose writings we have sometimes found such strong evidence of Old Testament views has also said quite clearly (1 Cor. 6) that in his opinion it is good for men and women to marry, but that it is better for both to remain unmarried; and he has frequently praised the achievement of women in the first Christian Churches.

Before passing on to examine the vocation of men and women to the service of God, we would consider whether, according to the order of nature, professions should be distributed between the sexes in such a way that some would be reserved to men, others to women, (and still others might be open to both). In my view this question, too, has to be answered in the negative. For there are strong individual differences, so that some women closely approach the masculine, and some men the feminine type. Hence every 'masculine' profession may also be very satisfactorily filled by certain women, and every 'feminine' one by certain men. Therefore I do not think legal barriers should be erected in this matter, but adequate education and vocational guidance should aim at a suitable choice of profession and eliminate undesirable elements by insisting on the necessary qualifications. For the average man and woman a division between the professions will come about quite normally, since evidently, owing to their natural differences, they will be suited for different kinds of work. Physical strength, predominantly abstract reasoning or independent creative work will be required in the 'masculine' professions, that is in heavy manual work, industry, agriculture; in the exact sciences such as mathematics, physics and technology; further in mechanical offices and administrative work, and in certain—not in all—branches of art. A sphere for genuinely feminine work exists wherever sensibility, intuition and adaptability are needed, and where the whole human being needs attention, whether it has to be nursed or educated or helped in any other way, perhaps by understanding it and assisting it to express itself. This means that a woman will find congenial work in the teaching and the medical professions, in all kinds of social work, in those branches of scholarship whose object is man and his activities, and in the arts that represent men; but also in business, in national and communal administration insofar as these have to deal mainly with people.

In times of extreme economic stress like our own* a natural distribution of men and women among the professions will not be feasible, since everyone has to seize whatever chance of employment there is, whether it be suited to his specific and individual talents or not. At present it is almost the rule that people have jobs that are not congenial; it is almost a particular 'stroke of luck' if it is otherwise. In such cases no more can be done than to make the best of the existing situation. On the one hand we have to satisfy the professional demands made on us, on the other we shall try not to let our own nature starve by denying its needs, but to make it as profitable as possible in the circle in which we are placed. For a woman this may mean, for example, that she will show herself sympathetic and helpful to her colleagues in a mechanical job; for a man that he will bring his inventive abilities to bear on the organization of his work. This, it is true, demands a high measure of personal maturity and a good will that is ready to adapt itself to any situation and to give its best in it. Such an attitude can hardly be achieved unless we regard the circumstances of our life as given by God and the work as His service, in which we are to develop the gifts He has bestowed on us in His honour. This is true of every profession, not only of the one styled 'consecrated to God', though it is there of course especially evident.

* This was written in the early thirties, shortly before the advent of Hitler, when unemployment in Germany had reached catastrophic dimensions. Ed.

Of priests and religious we say in common parlance that they must have a special 'vocation', that is to say that they must have received a particular call from God. Is there a difference between men and women in this sphere? At all times both men and women have been called to the religious state. If today we consider the manifold forms of contemporary religious life, the charitable activities to which also the feminine Orders and Congregations are devoted, there remains really only the one essential difference that the specifically priestly work is reserved to men. This brings us to the difficult and much discussed question of the priesthood of women.*

If we consider our Lord's own attitude in this respect, we shall find that He accepted from women the free services of love both for Himself and for His disciples, and that women were among His most intimate friends; but He did not give them the priesthood, not even to His Mother, the Queen of Apostles, who surpassed all mankind in human perfection and in the fullness of grace. In the primitive Church women were engaged in manifold charitable activities, the female confessors and martyrs exercized a fruitful apostolate; there existed a liturgical consecration of virgins and also the diaconate of women with a special ordination—but never a feminine priesthood. In the course of the later historical development women were progressively eliminated from all ecclesiastical offices. Their position in canon law gradually deteriorated, probably under the influence of the Old Testament and Roman legal customs. In the most recent times we have been witnessing a change, owing to the powerful demand for women helpers in charitable and parochial work. There is a desire among women that these activities should once more be given the character of a sacred ecclesiastical order, and it is quite possible that one day this wish may be fulfilled. But it is questionable whether this would be the first step on the way that would ultimately lead to the priesthood of women. It seems to me that from the doctrinal point of view there would be no obstacle forbidding the Church to introduce such a hitherto unheard-of innovation. From the practical point of view several

* Discussed especially in Germany between the wars though scarcely in other countries. Ed.

reasons both for and against it might be adduced. Against it would be the entire tradition from the first times until now, and, in my view, even more the mysterious fact which I have stressed before: that Christ appeared on earth as the *Son* of Man, that therefore the first Creature on earth that was made in an eminent sense after the image of God was a Man. This seems to me to point to the fact that He wanted to appoint only men to be His official representatives on earth. Nevertheless, He united Himself to *one* woman as closely as to no other creature on earth; He created her after His own image in such a way as no other human being either before or after, and gave her for all eternity an unrivalled position in the Church. In a similar way He has at all times called women to the most intimate union with Himself, to be apostles of His love, to announce His will to kings and Popes, to prepare His kingdom in the hearts of men. There is no higher vocation than to be a spouse of Christ, and a woman who sees this way open before her will desire no other.

However, to belong to God and to serve Him in the free surrender of love is not the vocation of a few chosen ones, but of every Christian. Every one of us, whether consecrated or not, whether man or woman, is called to follow Christ. The further he progresses in this way, the more Christlike he will become. Now Christ embodies the ideal of human perfection, in Him there are no defects, the advantages of the male and female natures are united in Him, the weaknesses abolished. Therefore His faithful disciples will also be increasingly elevated above the limitations of their nature: in saintly men we see tender gentleness and a truly motherly care for the souls entrusted to them, in women manly courage, firmness and decision. Thus if we follow Christ we shall be led to fulfil our original human vocation. We shall mirror God in us, the Master of Creation, by protecting and preserving all creatures in our care, the Father, by generating and forming children for His Kingdom in spiritual fatherhood and motherhood. But this transcending of natural barriers is the highest effect of grace; it can never be achieved by carrying on a self-willed struggle against nature and denying its barriers, but only by humble subjection to the divine order.

B. From PROBLEMS OF WOMEN'S EDUCATION

We understand by education or culture the formation of a being destined for development, whether this is achieved by a spontaneous process from within, through spontaneously effective external influences, or by the person's own and other people's deliberate educational efforts. If this be so it is obviously indispensable for understanding this process to know what it is that is being formed. If we restrict education to planned educational work it is a fundamental practical requirement to know the material on which this is to be done.

If we have a class of schoolchildren before us it will be obvious at the first glance that not two of them are alike. Nor do we only notice external differences, but at the same time internal ones (though we cannot here explain what this latter perception means, and which external differences are especially important for the diagnosis of interior ones): as many human beings, as many individuals, that is to say beings of their own special kind. When we come to know them by longer acquaintance they will form themselves into groups for us, which are united to each other by typical traits which they have in common, and separated from each other by those in which they differ. The individuals will now appear as representatives of a type. Apart from the types that appear in the same age group, there are types characteristic of a certain age which will become obvious as soon as different forms are compared with each other. (To this is added the type of a form, which is to be carefully distinguished from the age type). We will leave aside for the moment the question of what causes these types, several of which may overlap in one individual. If we compare a class of girls with one of boys, we shall again find typical differences. The question now is, whether we are here concerned with types in the same sense as with a girls' or a boys' form, or whether we have met a universality of a new kind, which is at the root of the types in either case. I have

formerly spoken of woman as a species. By species we here understand something permanent, that does not change. For this
Thomist philosophy also uses the term form, meaning an interior
form that determines the structure of a thing. The type is not
immutable in the same sense as the species. An individual for
example may pass from one type to another. This happens in
the process of development, in which the individual representing
the type of the child progresses into that of the young person and
of the adult. This progress is enjoined on him by an inner form.
A child can also change its type if it passes from one class to
another (that is among other children) or from one family into
another. Such changes are attributed to the influence of its
environment. Yet insofar as an interior form exists, such
influence has its limits. The inner form or species circumscribes
a sphere within which the types may vary. It is surely evident
that the question of the species 'woman' concerns the principle
of all women's questions. If such a species exists, then it cannot
be affected by any change of conditions, of the economic and
cultural situation as well as of one's own occupation. If there is
no such species, if 'man' and 'woman' are not to be regarded as
species but only as types in the sense that has just been defined,
then it is possible, in certain circumstances, to change from one
type into the other. This is not so absurd as it may seem at the
first glance. This view has been defended in the form that the
physical differences are accepted as permanent, whereas the
psychological ones are taken to be infinitely variable; but even
against the immutability of the physical differences certain facts
such as hermaphrodites and intermediary forms may be adduced.

This question of principle in women's problems points back
to the principles of philosophy. In order to be able to answer it
satisfactorily we must be clear about the relations between genus,
species, type and individual, that is about the fundamental
problems of formal ontology, in which I see what was envisaged
by Aristotle in his concept of the 'first philosophy'. The matters
that are clarified by this fundamental discipline in their formal
generality will have to be examined in detail by material disciplines for their special subjects. The inquiry into the being of

woman has its logical place in a philosophical anthropology. It is part of the doctrine of man to clarify the meaning of the sexual differentiation, to work out the content of the species, and the position of the species in the structure of the human individual, as well as the relation of the types to the species and the individual, and the conditions under which types are formed.

It is a necessary foundation for practical educational work to be clear about the demands and the limitations of the species, to know with what types and individuals one has to reckon in a given case, and in what way they can be influenced. A person may have this concrete fundamental knowledge for the practical work in the education of girls without the total theoretical preparatory work having been done either at all, or by the teacher personally. But it should be evident that if the educational work is built on false theories, this must also lead to mistakes in its practice.

How, then, are we to set about laying the theoretical foundations of the education of girls? Or where shall we take our terms of reference for selecting suitable material for a solid foundation from the flood of the existing literature on women's questions? We have to ask ourselves what are the ways of knowledge at our disposal, and if we would form an opinion on an existing examination of the subject, we must first find out the end it has in view, the method it has followed, and whether its end could be, and actually has been, attained by it.

There is a purely scientific method of treating the special properties of woman. This is used by anatomy and physiology, which describe and explain the structure and functions of the female body on experimental lines. This is also the method of scientific or elementary psychology. By means of observation and experiment it examines individual psychological data of the greatest possible number of cases and endeavours to derive from these general laws of psychological behaviour. In the beginning of the twentieth century sex psychology, too, has followed these lines. The individual psychical performances of a number of persons of either sex and the qualities revealed by them were investigated; for example the receptivity of the senses, the ability to learn and memorize, talent for certain subjects, special inclinations such as are revealed e.g. in people's favourite games and occupations, peculiarities of the imagination, of mind and will, etc. All these scientific investigations presuppose the difference of sex as a universal fact of experience and strive to state as accurately as possible in what it consists. They arrive at describing the peculiarity by characteristics which are normally present, or the frequency, perhaps even the degree, of which can be numerically established. They fail, however, to achieve a universally valid presentation of the special property, and, even more, to decide whether this property is to be regarded as a variable type or as a permanent species.

In the first years of this century psychology underwent an important change. Elementary psychology has been increasingly relegated to the background in favour of another type, which has been called 'understanding', 'structural' or *geisteswissenschaftlich*.* In this, several different branches would have to be distinguished; but they all have in common that they apprehend the life of the *psyche* as a unified whole which cannot be divided into, and put together from, its elements. (In the beginning scientific pychologists liked to speak of the 'psychology without the soul' or left it at least doubtful whether a unity really existed behind the individual psychological facts. Even in the *geisteswissenschaftliche* psychology this scepticism with regard to the substantial existence of the soul is by no means a thing of the past). The representatives of structural psychology, especially those called individual psychologists, are convinced that the individual psychological facts—individual actions, achievements, and also qualities—cannot be understood apart from the psychological make-up from which they spring, within which they run their course, and the progress of which they themselves partly determine. Hence its task must be to grasp, understand and interpret the whole, in order to see the individual facts in their context. Now, since this new method came into existence in order to meet the needs of the *Geisteswissenschaften* (history, literature etc.) as well as those

---

* an almost untranslatable word coined to distinguish those branches of scholarship dealing with philosophy, history, languages etc., from the natural sciences. Ed.

of the diagnosis and cure of psychological abnormalities, and since in both cases it is a question of understanding certain individual personalities, the description of individual psychological contexts *(Gesamtzusammenhaenge)* plays a prominent part in it. The material for this is supplied by experiences from one's own personal life, from the educational and psychiatric practice, and from diaries and memoirs.

Nevertheless, it proved impossible to stop short at the description of individuals; first, because every description has to make use of the concept of types, for the individuality as such cannot be grasped by concepts; secondly, because the material reveals certain types; the structural *ensemble* is neither merely universal, i.e. the same in all men without any differentiation, nor is it merely individual, unique in each one without having anything in common with the others; and because the types are practically important, supply methods of influencing pupils and patients. Hence this form of psychology necessarily came across the feminine 'type', or rather, a variety of feminine types. Now since individual psychology could not be satisfied with a momentary survey of the psychological life, but had to aim at grasping, if possible, its whole development, it escaped the danger of taking the types it found for something rigid and permanent. It was too obvious that they changed with changing external circumstances. Moreover, if we concentrate on the personality as a whole, we shall be led to take the soul in its psycho-somatic unity. Now, as the human person always exists in the world, which also constantly determines its psychological behaviour, psychology must needs pass beyond itself to anthropological, sociological and cosmological considerations. This has been very clearly expressed by Rudolf Allers in his treatise on *Sexual Psychology as a Precondition of Sexual Pedagogics* (Muenster, 1931). As he rightly emphasizes, the educationist must strive to investigate in how far the types are capable of change and hence of undergoing his influence. He may not stop short too soon before a supposedly 'unalterable disposition', but must try to see every form of conduct as a reaction to external circumstances which, under different circumstances, might take a different form. That which lies beyond the limit this method reveals, which resists all influence, Allers wants to be regarded as an irrational residue which he calls X. If we apply this to our own problem, it would mean that the existence of a species is not denied, but that its contents could not be grasped; hence its share in the formation of a type and in the conduct of a person could not be determined, and there would be no basis on which to establish educational practice. It seems to me unduly pessimistic to apply this confession of ignorance not only to *Individualpsychologie* but to knowledge as such. Here, it is true, the boundary of empirical psychology seems to have been reached. Like every other positive science—and by this I mean a science of natural facts based on natural experience,—it can only state that in certain circumstances a thing is in such and such a condition and reacts, or must react, in such and such a way. These sciences do not attain to the inner form and to the ontological structure of the cosmos as such, which causes events in the world to be what the positive sciences say they are.

Now the problems of philosophy begin where the work of the positive sciences leaves off. It is not allowed to be content with the X of an unknowable 'natural disposition'. I would contend that philosophy is capable of analyzing three things in this X, though these are separable only by abstraction, not in reality. These are, first, the species of man (whether it would be more suitable here to speak of genus or of species could be decided only after examining the formal ontological problem), second the species of woman, and third, individuality.

This brings us face to face with the great question of philosophical method. Within our context it is impossible to develop it in its whole range and to derive a method from ultimate sources. We have to be content to indicate the ways which, in our opinion are capable of leading to the solution of the problems that have been raised. With the phenomenological school (that is the school of E. Husserl) I share the view that the method of philosophy differs in principle from that of the positive sciences. Philosophy has its own function of knowledge, which enables it to do what is necessary for the foundation of the other branches of scholarship and what these latter cannot do themselves, namely to define the domain of their subject and to reveal the means and methods of knowledge adapted to it. Phenomenology has called this peculiar function of knowledge intuition or *Wesensanschauung*. These terms, however, have had a long history and have therefore often been misinterpreted. I understand by this the achievement of knowledge *(Erkenntnisleistung)* which brings out the general structure of concrete objects, enabling us, for example, to say what is a material thing, a plant, an animal, or a man, and what is the meaning of these terms. What is here called intuition is closely related to what traditional philosophy calls abstraction. A thorough phenomenological analysis of intuition and abstraction could perhaps show that it is useless to argue which of the two is the true philosophical method. The relevance of this for our own question should be obvious: it is possible to give meaning to such terms as 'essence of woman' or 'species of woman' only, if there exists a function of knowledge capable of bringing out universal characteristics. Most writers on this subject began their work without even raising the question of method (as far as they did not remain within the framework of positive science). They wrote from their 'feeling' or 'instinct'. By this we would not imply that this whole literature is worthless. It has the same value as any other pre-scientific experience and theory, the value of material that has critically to be worked out and sifted. Everyone knows women by experience and hence thinks he knows what a woman is. But if he draws a general picture from his experiences we cannot be sure whether this is not a faulty generalization, whether what has actually been observed in certain cases does not fail to be true for others. Moreover, the individual experience itself has to be critically examined. Has even the individual woman been properly understood? All experiences are subject to error and deception, and here this danger is perhaps greater than elsewhere. Where shall we find a guarantee that it has been avoided? Or perhaps we are presented with an ideal picture of woman, which serves as a standard by which to ascertain whether others are 'true' women. Then again we shall have to ask whence this ideal picture has been taken and what value it has to increase our knowledge. Now one point has to be detached from all these considerations as particularly important, that is the claim to be able to make general statements. Without realizing it, people assume quite naively that they grasp something universal in their individual experiences. Hence the philosopher has the task to bring out the general function of knowledge effective in experience, to systematize it, and thus to raise it to the rank of a scientific method.

I must once more refrain from discussing in detail how far this way of knowledge has already been investigated. I only want to single out one book from the flood of literature written by both men and women on the being and nature of woman, because it is serious, scholarly, and, as it seems to me, a pioneer work. Since its publication (Freiburg, Herder, 1932) it has already been widely discussed. It is called *Seinsrhythmik* (The Rhythm of Being), A Study for the Foundation of a Metaphysics of the Sexes, its author is Sister Thoma Angelica Walter of the Poor Child Jesus. It opens up a completely new way to find the ultimate sense of the terms masculine and feminine. The problem of the sexes has been reduced to its radical ontological form, i.e. she examines whether masculine and feminine are not basic forms of being, in fact a double form appearing in all created being. These fundamental forms are pursued through all the stages of created being, from the first creature, light, to the highest spiritual creatures. The work owes its fundamental importance to the wide sweep of its problem and the certainty and vigour of the ontological treatment. I am also convinced that it contains lasting results; nevertheless I must add that the author fails to justify the method she employs, and this seems to me the reason why not all her conclusions can be regarded as indisputable. She is guided by certain fundamental truths taken from the philosophy of St. Thomas Aquinas, as well as some statements from the writings of E. Przywara and R. Guardini. Besides, she uses a method approaching the phenomenological intuition. Finally, she occasionally utilizes results of recent research from various sciences such as mathematics, physics and biology. But she fails to justify the combination of these various methods, and

133

to discuss their relation to each other. This, indeed, could only have been done if the treatise on the problem of the sexes had been preceded by a special system of philosophy. In the short methodical preliminaries contained in the Foreword of the book, the author states that it is founded on the Catholic faith as the surest system of human knowledge. But she does not work out separately what has been said about the problem of the sexes in this quarter.

With this we have reached the last method of dealing with our question that is still to be discussed, namely the theological one. It is of fundamental importance to us to know what Catholic doctrine says about the essence and nature of woman. This we shall seek first in doctrine in the narrowest sense, that is in everything we are bound to believe, in the dogmatic definitions. What we shall find there will not amount to much. We shall then go farther afield and try to ascertain the traditional teaching, adducing the writings of the Doctors and Fathers of the Church and of the dogmatic treatises of the present. Here we shall find more abundant material, though a material that allows of criticism. If St. Thomas says, for example, "The man is the origin and end of the woman" (*Summa Theologica* 1, quest. 92, art. 1) we shall ask ourselves what is the meaning of this sentence and from what source it has been taken. In this case the latter question is not difficult to answer. The source of the statement is the creation account of Holy Scripture; some passages from St. Paul are also relevant. In order to define its meaning, it would first have to be ascertained from the context of Thomist thought what he means by calling one thing the principle and end of another. We should further have to take into account all Scriptural passages from which a definition of the end of woman could be derived (and analogously something about her 'secondary' position in relation to man); what results from these as principle and end would then have to be compared with the statement of Thomas that has just been cited. Supposing the meaning of both were identical, we should further have to ask what would follow from the end and position of woman for her nature. For it is clear that, if woman was created for a certain purpose, her nature would have to be adapted to that. The types which we know from experience could then be opposed to the nature as it appears from this indirect way of knowledge. If we find divergences we should have to ask how such a falling away from nature was possible and how it is to be explained. Moreover, if we should have arrived at grasping the essence of woman by purely philosophical insight, this directly apprehended essence would have to be opposed to her nature such as it has been deduced from theological considerations. If there should be discrepancies, this could be attributed to error on either side. It might, however, also be possible that the meanings of the terms 'nature' and 'essence' *(Wesen)* are not altogether identical. This is an ontological problem which we will not here elaborate.

Finally, the discussion of the theological opinions has led to another way of theological investigation, to which the dogmatic treatment refers back, namely the treatment of what Scripture itself reveals. I have made a small beginning in the treatise *The Vocation of Man and Woman according to the Orders of Nature and of Grace,* by attempting to collect and interpret some passages that seemed important to me. But it would be a great and rewarding task to work through the whole of the Bible with this point in view.

We have now recorded a series of different methods by which one has tried, or could try, to find out the peculiar characteristics of woman. We would now once more summarize what each of them according to the means of knowledge at its disposal, can contribute to our problem. To elucidate the species corresponds to the proper noetic function of philosophy, which alone is capable of achieving it. In order at least to give a hint how I visualize the solution of this, I must place it within the whole context of philosophical problems such as I see it. As I have already said elsewhere, I consider ontology to be the fundamental discipline, i.e. the theory of the basic forms of being and of beings. This is able to show that there is a radical division within being. On the one hand we have pure being, which contains nothing of non-being, has neither beginning nor end, and contains all that is capable of being; on the other we have finite being, which begins and comes to an end, this being characteristic of all finite being. We call the one uncreated, the other created being. The Creator corresponds to the former, creatures to the latter. These terms are taken from the language of theology, but what they signify can be demonstrated by purely philosophical methods. The creatures can be arranged in grades, according to whether they approach pure being more or less closely. For all creaturely being is analogous to the divine Being. This analogy of being, however, differs for each stage. A different kind of being and a different fundamental form of beings correspond to each of these stages, which are material, organic, animal and spiritual being. Man holds a particular place in this graduated edifice, because all lower grades are contained in his structure. His body is material, but not only that. At the same time it is an organism formed and active from within. Again, man is not only an organism, but endowed with a soul, sensitive in a special way and aware of himself and his surroundings. Finally, he is a spiritual being, endowed with knowledge both of himself and others, and capable of creative activity. All this belongs to the species man, and nothing that does not show this structure can be called 'man'. Now this species appears as differentiated in individuals: every human being has his own unrepeatable peculiarity, notwithstanding his specific human nature. Philosophy can show that individuality, in the sense of uniqueness, belongs to the species man, but it is outside its scope to grasp such and such an individual. This belongs to a specific function of experience which we use in our relations with men. Another, simple differentiation cuts across this differentiation of humanity into an unlimited multiplicity of individuals: this is the difference of sex.

The author of the aforementioned book on *Seinsrhythmik* attempts to pursue this differentiation through all the stages of being. She stresses as the property of all created being that its existence can be distinguished from that which it is, and that its existence must have a duration in time in order to develop that which it is. Mother Thoma Angelica distinguishes terminologically between 'existence' and 'being such' *(Dasein und Sosein).*

I shall explain presently that my principal objection is directed only against building on this pair of oppositions. A specific rhythm corresponds to the 'power of being' *(Seinsmacht)* of every being, which in this rhythm develops what it is *(sein Was)* in its existence. This rhythm is different in each stage, and, according to Mother Thoma Angelica, it is always a double one, according to what prevails: that which wants to take a form by existing, or the existence which wants to take a form. The existence-component is viewed as female, the component of 'being such' as male. All creatures combine both. The preponderance of the fullness of existence is taken to be the specific characteristic of the female, the preponderance of the creative power as that of the male rhythm of being. In the lower ranges of creatures we have not yet two parallel lines of forms, that is not yet the actual sexual differentiation as it begins to appear in the realm of organic existence, but forms that show neither the one nor the other rhythm of being. Where the species (of plants or animals) exhibits the double form, it is itself to be regarded as the unity consisting of both partial species. This unity finds its strongest expression in the fact that the species is propagated and maintained in existence through the union of individuals in which the 'member rhythms' *(Gliedrhythmen)* are embodied. In man this double form appears not only in individuals of different member rhythm, but can be pursued also in every individual throughout his whole physical, psychological and spiritual structure. (Thus the will is regarded as a female, the reason as a male function of the soul). It is impossible to reproduce and criticize in detail how this rhythm of being is carried through. I would only say something about the ontological foundation which is the starting point of my reservations, and the effects of which are, of course, bound to show themselves even in the ultimate conclusions. The differentiation between 'existence' *(Dasein)* and 'being such *(Sosein)* is obviously meant to reproduce the Thomist one of existence and essence. Now the term 'being such' seems rather unfortunate to me, because it appears to be more suitable for the accidents than for the substantial form, which it is evidently meant to signify. For the accidents, too, one would have to distinguish further between 'thus' and 'being thus', that is between the accidental form and the being determined by the form. On the other hand, the term existence seems to contain much more than St. Thomas has put into it. If the whole work was meant to be guided by the Thomist ontology, then not only the pair 'essence' and 'existence', but also the two others of 'form' and 'matter', and 'act' and 'potency', ought to have been adduced. I had the impression that much that is ascribed to 'existence' would have been better suited to matter, and other things better to what is potential in beings *(fuer den potentiellen Bestand des Seienden)*. In my view the basis of an exact analysis of the whole ontological structure of created being is absolutely necessary to solve the problem whether 'male' and 'female' are really only to be taken as 'ryhthms of being', or if at the root of the different rhythm of being there is not rather a difference of the substantial form.

I would further mention the following questions as important for the education of girls. Is the difference between man and woman to be understood in such a way that the sexual differentiation cuts through the whole structure of man, or does this difference concern only the body and those psychological functions which are necessarily linked to physical organs, so that the mind would not be affected by it? This is a view held not only by many women, but also by certain theologians. If the second view could be maintained, the intellectual education could largely be carried on regardless of the sexual difference; in the opposite case educationists would have to reckon in their work with the specific intellectual structure. Further: if both male and female elements are contained in every individual and only the one or the other is predominant, would individuals of either 'species' be needed so as fully to represent the species man? Could it not be completely represented by one individual? This question, too, is of practical importance, because according to how it is answered education will have to aim either at overcoming or at developing the specific nature. In order to answer this question the whole complex of genetic problems would have to be examined; this has so far scarcely been touched. On the one hand, the actual form of human being *(Seinsweise des Menschen)* would have to be discussed: the species is not fully developed when it comes into existence, but causes the individual to develop progressively in a temporal process. This process follows no explicit rules, but depends on several variable factors, e.g. on the freedom of man that allows him to work on his own and other people's education. This property of human being is the cause why a multiplicity of types can come into existence, in which the species can take shape under varying conditions. Another genetical problem is the origin of new individuals, the transmission of the species through successive generations, and the increasing diversity of types in the course of history. In all this, philosophy is not concerned with the variations that have actually occurred in the life of an individual or in the course of history, but with those that are possible in principle. The connexion of the genetic problems with the problem of the development of the species may be expressed in the question whether perhaps the complete and concrete formation of the human species is possible only in the complete succession of the generations, and in the sexual as well as in the individual differentiation.

Whereas the specific noetic function of philosophy is to explore what is necessary and possible to beings according to their nature, theology has to ascertain what divine revelation tells us about the specific nature of woman. It has not to examine its objects themselves, but to collect and interpret the historical documents. The Word of Holy Scripture is not, as a rule, concerned with natural necessities and possibilities, but records facts and gives practical instructions. The philosopher asks, for example, whether the world had to start in time, or whether it is possible that it existed from eternity. The creation narrative says that it did begin in time and in what way. It does not ask whether the sexual differentiation is necessary or accidental, but says: "God created man to his own image . . . male and female he created them", expressing the fact of unity as well as of differentiation. But it is a concise saying requiring interpretation. What does the divine image in man signify? The whole history and doctrine of salvation gives the answer. It is summarized in the words of our Lord:

"Be ye perfect as your Father in heaven is perfect". I will not at the moment discuss the content of the ideal of perfection. I would only point out that through the imperative the divine image is presented as a task, as the vocation or destiny of man, that is to say of both man and woman. The theologian concludes from this that what is generally called 'woman's natural vocation' of wife and mother cannot be her only one. It is true, this 'natural vocation' is also expressed in Scripture. The destiny of the wife is affirmed in the words that give the reason of woman's creation: "It is not good for man to be alone"; the call to motherhood in the words: "Be fruitful and multiply". But beside this the New Testament proclaims the ideal of virginity; and notwithstanding the sanctity of marriage, it is of faith that the state of virginity is higher than the married state. Hence from this point of view, too, it is impossible, if we profess the Catholic faith, to consider marriage and motherhood to be her only vocation.

I cannot enlarge any further on the material that might be adduced from theology, and especially from Holy Scripture, for discussing the problem of the sexes. But I think even these examples show that we have here the firm foundation of certain facts and norms. Though by no means all we can and should like to know is contained in revelation, and though reason is left a wide field for its research, yet, if we thoroughly drain this Scriptural source we shall be saved from many errors in theory as well as in practice. If both the theological and the philosophical ways of thinking be rightly understood and used, they will be found not to compete with, but to complement and fertilize each other, according to the well-known sayings: "I believe that I may understand" and "Faith seeking understanding". The data of faith demand that philosophizing reason should make them intelligible as far as possible. On the other hand, they protect it from error and answer certain questions of fact that reason must leave undecided.

The positive sciences, occupied with stating natural facts, are in a similar position. Physiology can tell us about the actual physical capacity of girls and lay down rules defining the demands that can be made on the various age groups as well as suggesting suitable exercizes to ensure good health, strength and ability. Elementary psychology can give valuable information on the actual performance of the memory, intellect etc. of girls. However, the importance of these facts can be gauged only if other considerations and statements are taken into account. It must be clear under which conditions the various tasks are performed, e.g. how they have been prepared by preceding exercizes. The whole character of the persons whose achievements are described has to be considered, as well as the milieu from which they come; that is to say elementary psychology has to be supplemented by *Individualpsychologie* and sociology. The former describes types with which we have to reckon and tries to make them intelligilble to us by showing up the connexions of motives within which the individual modes of conduct are placed. Thus Else Croner, in her book *Die Psyche der weiblichen Jugend* (The Psychology of Young Girls), Langensalza 1930, after first outlining the characteristics of the young girl as opposed to the child and the mature woman on the one hand, and to the young man on the other, proceeds to describe five types: The motherly girl will give clear indications of her interest in the child whether in her games, her favourite occupations or generally in her desires. The erotic type is predominantly interested in men and shows signs of being highly sexed. The romantic girl desires 'experiences' and wants to surrender herself entirely to a 'leader', perhaps without any suggestion of sex. Girls of the fourth type are sober, interested in practical tasks and easily adapt themselves to varying conditions. Finally there is the intellectual type, predominantly concerned with objective interests and possibly capable of creative achievements. Those devoted to the education of girls will surely remember representatives of one or other of these types, and probably also mixed types or others than those mentioned. Such typological classification is useful for the teacher in various ways. It will sharpen his understanding of the human beings before him, though he will have to guard against a narrow systematization if he would do justice to the individuals. It will further remind us that we must take into account the diversity of human beings; that not all of them are open to everything, and that all cannot be formed to have the same ideals, that the ends as well as the ways and means have to be differentiated. On the other hand the types are not to be accepted as rigid natural data incapable of change. If individuals be observed over a longer period, taking into account various influences such as, for example, different teachers and tutors or decisive changes of milieu, say from the family into a boarding school or from school into a job, we shall often notice the transition of one type to another. Experiences in the training and treatment of abnormal or at least 'difficult' young people will supply valuable material on the possibility of influencing the types, as will also a historical survey, which would show a predominance of various types in certain circumstances, as well as the appearance of new types and possibly the disappearance of old ones. The fact that they can be influenced makes it necessary to consider aims and values. It will have to be asked which types deserve to be preserved and which demand an education aiming at transforming them; moreover it will also have to be considered which types can be set up as ends, that is to say into which existing ones ought to be changed.

After these lengthy methodical considerations which would show how we can come to know the 'material' that is to be educated, I will try quickly to sketch that with which we are concerned in the education of girls. This is done by anticipation, as it were, because we have found everywhere a multitude of unsolved problems. I can only outline the picture as it presents itself to me at the moment. Further studies will no doubt greatly enrich and perhaps also modify it.

I am convinced that the human species develops as a double species of 'man' and 'woman', that the human essence in which no trait should be missing shows a twofold development, and that its whole structure has this specific character. There is a difference not only of bodily structure and of certain physiological functions, but the whole somatic life is different, as well as the relation of soul and body; and within the psychological sphere there is a similar difference of the relationship between intellect and sensuality and between the various intellectual faculties. The female species is characterized by the unity and wholeness of the entire psycho-somatic personality and by the harmonious development of the faculties; the male species by the perfecting of individual capacities to obtain record achievements.

This differentiation of the species as worked out by philosophy corresponds to the destiny of the sexes shown by theology. Man and woman are destined to have dominion over the earth, i.e. to know and enjoy the things of this world, and to form them by creative action. But these cultural tasks are assigned in the first place to man; woman is given him as his helper. Both, man and woman, are meant to produce and educate posterity. Nevertheless, this is predominantly the task of woman, being physically and psychologically more closely united to the child, and through this union more restricted in her whole way of life, whereas man is placed by her side to help and protect her. Her particular way of knowledge corresponds to her task of being companion and mother. Her strength is the intuitive grasp of the living concrete, especially of the personal element. She has the gift of making herself at home in the inner world of others, of entering into their aims and ways of work. Feeling *(Gemüt)* holds the central place in her life, enabling her to grasp and appreciate concrete being in its proper quality and specific value. She desires to develop the human personality as perfectly as possible, and her whole life is governed by 'eros' (by which we do not mean sexuality), the purest flower of which is serving love. Both man and woman are destined to show forth the image of God. It is part of their finite being that they have to do this, too, in a specific way. One difference has already been indicated: woman reproduces the divine perfection more by the harmonious development of all her powers, man by the more pronounced development of particular faculties. It would also be possible to show their difference in the relation to the attributes of God and to the divine Persons.

The species—humanity as well as femininity—is differently expressed in different individuals. For one thing, they realize the species more or less perfectly; besides, they show the various characteristics more or less pronouncedly. Man and woman have the same fundamental human characteristics, some of which predominate not only in the sexes, but also in individuals.

Therefore women may closely approach the masculine type and *vice versa*. This may be due to their individual vocation. If marriage and motherhood are the primary vocation of the female sex as such, this need not be the case for each individual. Women may be destined for special cultural achievements, and their natural gifts may be adapted to these. Thus we arrive at feminine types classified according to their natural endowments. Because human nature is finite, the vocation to create culture is split up into a variety of professions. Hence the desire for perfection, too, though all men are called to it, may become a special vocation, as happens in the religious Orders. This vocation, which includes the vocation to virginity, will be suited to a feminine type for whom close human relationships such as belong to marriage and motherhood hold a second place. Such women will realize the fundamental personal attitude and the predominance of 'eros' in its highest form of the love of God which will fashion their lives. Each individual has its place and task in the one great develop-ment of mankind, which should be seen as a single Individual. (The history of the Redemption can be understood only on this presupposition). Each individual human being is a member of this whole, showing its structure; but at the same time it has its own character as a member, which it must develop if the whole is to develop. The species man is perfectly realized only in the course of the world's history, in which the great individual Mankind becomes concrete. The species man and woman, too, can be fully realized only in this total development. Whoever is engaged in educational work is given material which he must help to form to that membership to which it is called.

The types and individuals are not solely determined by being members within the whole of mankind. We cannot understand the material before us and the tasks it imposes on us unless we take into account the fact of original sin. All that is called 'disease', 'abnormality', 'difficult to educate' ultimately stems from this source. Just as the nature of fallen man differs from that of man in his original integrity, so the nature of man and woman and of each individual is tainted by sin. All human educa-tional work has the task to co-operate in restoring the natural integrity. Fallen man is characterized by two fundamental traits, the rebellion of the spirit against the dominion of God, and the revolt of the lower powers against the higher, of the senses against the spirit, of the will against reason. The former brings about a change in man's relationship to the other creatures, which he wants to exploit for himself instead of preserving them for God. The lower creatures react by revolting against man, hence there arises a state of war. The rebellion of the senses and the spirit results in the loss of direction of either (deceit, error and practical fault) with all its harmful consequences for body and soul. This is true both for man and woman. The specific perversions of man are a brutal despotism that shows itself in the treatment of all creatures and especially of woman, and an enslavement by his work that may paralyze his humanity. The specific perversions of woman are a slavish attachment to man and absorption of the spirit in the sensual life of the body. This may show itself in various types. It is most evident in the one E. Croner calls 'erotic', but which should rather be termed 'sexual'. Women of this type are exclusively interested in the sexual sphere, which often captivates their imagination in their early youth, in any case from the beginning of puberty. Their whole behaviour will change in the presence of men. They have strong, uncontrolled instincts which make them an easy prey to seduction and finally to prostitution. In the 'romantic type' all this is transposed into a more spiritual and ideal sphere. Girls of this type will be given to daydreaming and inventing imaginary heroes; they will live with them in a phantom world, and thus their power of judgement and their capacity for real life will be impaired. We have further the type of the rebellious slave, the emancipated woman who rejects not only slavish ties, but also the subjection willed by God, and takes up a fighting position against men, betraying by this attitude the existence of just such ties. Other types might be added to these. In the soberly practical and objectively intellectual types mentioned above, this latter form of perversion is obviously to be feared less. It might, however, also be argued that this advantage is linked to a weakness, namely to the poor development of the integral feminine nature.

If those types and individuals which are to be considered differentiations of the pure human nature give us positive directives for our educational work, the perverted types need measures designed to reform them. The girls we have before us are not inescapably imprisoned in the type which they represent at the moment. If today the sexual type is more frequent than perhaps twenty years ago, this is certainly due to external influences which make even children acquainted with this subject and encourage dispositions which otherwise would never come into the open. If the romantic type was frequent in the past, this was no doubt partly due to the whole atmosphere of the life of girls and women. They were farther removed from real life; feminine education was quite different, and the influence of teenager literature, novels that were themselves written by women of the romantic type, and of the feminine ideal of romantic men also played a decisive part. If today the soberly practical type is definitely in the ascendance, this is no doubt for the greater part due to the stiff demands of modern life.

It will then be the task of the educationist to create conditions suited to counteract perversions, and to contribute to restoring nature in its integrity.

In surveying the present situation of women we have met the demands our time makes on girls' education. When considering the material with which this educational effort has to reckon, this appeared to be determined by a goal. In planning our work we cannot try to realize both these demands side by side, but have to weigh them against each other in order to envisage a homogenous end, though this may perhaps not be simple. Now a goal cannot be attained unless it is presented to the material as necessary or at least possible. Hence the demands of the time must be measured by those of eternity, that is by the eternal order of all being. Therefore we must first consider the aim or aims woman's nature and destiny demand.

We have seen that woman's nature has a threefold purpose: she is to develop her humanity, her femininity, and her individuality. These are no separate ends, just as the nature of the concrete human individual is not tripartite but one; it is the human nature in its specifically feminine and individual character. Only in abstract thought we have to consider separately what it notionally separated.

Whence do we take the idea of perfected humanity? It is the task of ethics to propose ends and demands, and to tell us what we ought to do. If we now had to construe ethics as a philosophical discipline, we should have critically to consider the question in how far an autonomous ethics, that is one resting on purely philosophical considerations unsupported by faith, would be capable of developing the idea of perfected humanity. If, however, we attempt to clarify the goal that is to be the norm of our educational work on the basis of faith, doctrinal truth, too, will belong to our theoretical foundations. We shall then start with the end of man proposed to us by faith, and adduce philosophical considerations only insofar as they are apt to elucidate the contents of faith intellectually or to supplement what faith leaves undecided.

Pius XI's encyclical *Rappresentanti* on the Christian education of youth states as "the true and immediate aim of Christian education . . . the co-operation with the grace of God in the formation of the true and perfect Christian, that is to say of Christ Himself in the person regenerated by baptism . . . The true Christian, therefore, the product of Christian education, is the supernatural man, who thinks, judges and acts always and consistently according to sound reason, enlightened by the supernatural light of the example and teaching of Christ; or, to use a contemporary expression, the true and perfect man of character. For not every kind of conduct displaying consistency and constancy according to purely subjective principles constitutes the true character, but perseverance in obeying the eternal principles of justice . . . On the other hand, perfect justice can exist only where the things of God are given to God, as is done by the true Christian".

We will here leave aside what is said about the forces working for the end, the grace of God and human co-operation, and confine ourselves to the end itself: that is the supernatural man, or Christ in man. This supernatural end does not exclude, but includes the natural end. "Hence the true Christian is far removed from resigning earthly activities or diminishing his natural capacities. On the contrary; by combining them with the supernatural life in orderly unity, he develops and perfects them, thus ennobling the natural life itself and adding to it more effective values not only of the spiritual and eternal, but also of the material and earthly world".

Thus in this brief formula natural and supernatural ends have been combined according to the axiom that grace perfects nature. If we would expand it, we must keep in mind the Christian teaching on nature before and after the fall and in its redeemed state. Now, this means developing all that is taught in the account of creation and fall, in the commandments, in the Gospel of Jesus Christ, and in the living example of the Godman.

The first man was created perfect; that is his nature was not meant to develop, but was mature and capable of all that is possible to human nature. For the moment we would leave aside the gifts that had been granted him by grace and those he was meant to receive in the state of glory. He was to transmit his pure nature to his descendants, not in its full maturity, but in germ, which was to reach its perfection in the course of their life. Adam's nature, therefore, was the end of the development. The integral nature such as it was before the fall, included the perfect strength, health and beauty of the body, the smooth functioning of all its organs, its unconditional obedience to the direction of the mind, that means the will enlightened by reason. The smooth functioning of the organs means at the same time impeccably functioning senses and infallible sense knowledge. The perfect condition of the mind means the creature's unerring rational knowledge of both creatures and Creator, a perfect harmony of reason and will; the latter, moreover, tends without hindrance towards the highest good, and the lower instincts are subject to the higher ends without resistance. It is to be asked, then, whether this pure human nature is also the end of our natural development, and has to be the end of our educational work. It is no longer the end of the human development in the same sense as before the fall, because our natural disposition is no longer sufficient to reach it, and may even resist it, though even fallen nature still tends in some way to this end. It must, however, be the end of our educational effort, though we are unable to reach it in its fullness by our own unaided efforts (we may only think, for example, of the perfect strength, health and beauty of the body). It can be attained only through grace, and in its perfection not until grace is perfected in glory. But we may not simply leave it to grace to lead fallen nature back to integrity, because justifying grace does not completely restore the integrity of nature, but only begins it and makes it possible on condition that we co-operate with it.

Adam was not only an integral man, but also the child of God, attracted to Him by faith and love, and knowing Him in a more perfect way than man does after the fall, called to see Him in the eternal vision, though not yet seeing Him directly. The immediate consequence of his turning away from God in the first sin was the loss of this childhood; another result was the loss of integrity, though the act of turning away already implied a fault against perfect justice. Hence it is the immediate end of Redemption to restore man to his state of a child of God, the restoration of the full integrity is a possible further effect of grace. To be a child of God and to reach the highest perfection of this state in the life of glory in heaven is the end proposed to us by the orders of creation and redemption, depending in both on our free co-operation. Therefore education must also include the supernatural end. It is through the redemptive work of Jesus Christ that man becomes once more a child of God, and is promised the beatific vision and the restoration of his nature. He gains access to this by personally attaching himself to the Godman. As a member of the mystical Body of Christ he is able by his own activity to co-operate in perfecting the redemptive work in himself and in the whole mystical Body under the guidance of its Head. Hence, if education envisages perfect humanity, it must aim at incorporation in the mystical Body.

Mankind has been created as a unique organism and has been restored to the organic form by union with Christ its Head. Each member has the one nature of the whole Body; but, being a member, it has its special character corresponding to its position in the organism. At the same time the whole Body shows a symmetrical structure: it is, as it were, a double being, whose complementary halves build up an harmonious whole and cause it to function. Education must aim at preserving for each member its character as such, and for the whole its symmetrical structure.

"Male and female he created them", creating woman for man as "a help as it were opposite him", according to the Hebrew text. She was to be his other half, in which he could see his own image and find himself. Together with him she was to take her place above all other creatures of the earth, none of which could be his equal, and was to build up the whole organism of mankind by producing posterity in union with him. This is the place to elucidate what St. Thomas means if he calls man "the principle and end of woman". First, a 'principle' is that from which another originates. Thus it signifies the fact that woman was made from man. It further signifies the first as the superior, to which the second is subject. This corresponds to the Pauline word that man is the head of woman. The 'end' is that to which another tends, where it finds rest and fulfilment. It expresses the fact that the meaning of feminine being is fulfilled in union with man. It further signifies all that for the sake of which another exists. It means that woman has been created for man, because he needs her in order to fulfil the meaning of his own being. I do not think that it means that woman was created only for the sake of man; for every creature has its own meaning, and that is its peculiar way of being an image of the divine being. For it was indeed quite possible to propagate mankind in another way than by the relation of the sexes, if this relation itself did not have its own meaning and value. Nor do I think the fact that woman was created 'for the sake of man' makes her inferior, unless it is misunderstood in the sense in which it could be misunderstood only after the perversion of both sexes through the fall, namely that she should serve as a means for man to fulfil his own ends and to pander to his lusts. This is not the purpose of the companion who was to be 'opposite him' above all other creatures.

She was meant to be his helpmate, enabling him by her own free decision to become what he was meant to be. For "neither is the man without the woman", therefore he must "leave father and mother and shall cleave to his wife".

Thus the education of girls should lead them to develop and affirm their proper feminine nature, and this includes the divinely willed vocation to live by the side of man, but not in his place, though neither in a humiliating position that would not be in keeping with the dignity of the human person.

It has already become evident that the meaning of the specifically feminine way of being is not solely to be understood from the relation between man and woman. Since this is closely connected with the propagation of the race, the special relation of woman to posterity must also be taken into account. It has, moreover, already been emphasized that all creaturely being stands in an image-relation to the Godhead; hence feminine being, too, must have a special image function. Finally it will have to be asked whether this ultimate sense of feminine being can only be realized in marriage and motherhood, or also in some other way.

From the creation narrative we learn only that man and woman together are called to propagate the race. We can gather only from the punishment after the fall, which inflicts the painful pangs of birth on woman, that she is allotted a special task in this. The punishment of man, on the other hand, is not connected with the relationship to posterity, but with that to the other creatures. Eve is called 'mother of the living' and rejoices when God has given her a son. In Israel mothers of children, especially of sons, were honoured and praised, whereas the childless woman was despised and regarded as subject to a curse. Thus the Psalmist counts it a special proof of the goodness of God that He made the barren woman a happy mother (Ps. 112). The position of the wife and mother in the family is highly esteemed. Her reputation transcends the confines of her home. She looks after the well-being of her house and all its inhabitants, but also opens her hands to the poor; the heart of her husband confides in her. Even the grown-up sons look up to her and listen to her advice. "She opens her mouth unto wisdom, and the law of clemency is on her tongue". (Proverbs 31 : 26). She deserves praise, because she fears the Lord. This is the secret of her efficiency and success. Where, in Jewish families, something of the Old Testament tradition is still alive, there a woman still holds this royal position. It is her honourable task not only to bring children into the world and look after their physical development, but also to bring them up in the fear of the Lord. This high esteem of motherhood is due to the consoling promise given to the first woman when she was driven from paradise, that she and her seed were destined to crush the head of the serpent. It has been the vocation of woman to fight against evil and educate her children to do the same, from the fall till the time of the Mother whose Son overcame death and hell, and it will have to remain so until the end of the world.

At the turning point of history, and especially of the history of woman, stands the woman in whom motherhood has been transfigured and at the same time, as physical motherhood, overcome. If Christ is the concrete goal of all human education, Mary is the end of the education of women. The fact that on the threshold between the Old and the New Covenants the new Eve stands by the side of the new Adam, is the clearest proof that the distinction of the sexes has an eternal significance and value. When God became incarnate He chose to be born from a human mother and presented us with the perfect image of a Mother. From the moment she knows that she is going to give birth to a son, she devotes herself completely to this vocation. He has been given her by God, and she must preserve Him for God. Her life is recollected expectancy till the hour of His birth, and then surrendered in service, listening to all the words and signs indicating something of His future life. Though venerating the hidden Godhead, she yet preserves her maternal authority while He is a child, later takes her share in His work and remains with Him in His death and beyond it. Yet this woman, who was called to the highest form of motherhood, had, before the annunciation of her election, resigned marriage and motherhood, contrary to the whole tradition of her people. She was determined to live free from sexual relationship. Being 'the handmaid of the Lord', she gave birth to the Son of God and obeyed the man who was placed by her side to protect herself and the child. She did not become 'one flesh' with him; this marriage was not meant to perpetuate His race and the human race in general. In Mary we meet the image of virginal purity. What else could have prompted her decision to remain unmarried, but the desire to be wholly 'the handmaid of the Lord', to belong to Him alone, completely at His disposal? And how could such a desire be explained except by divine inspiration and vocation?

Thus she leaves the natural order and joins the Redeemer as Co-Redemptress. Both spring from the human race, both embody the human nature; yet both are free from that relationship which enables a man to fulfil the meaning of his life only in and through union with another. In both this is replaced by union with God; in Christ through the hypostatic union, in Mary through the complete surrender of her whole being to the service of the Lord. It might be asked if both are so utterly separated from the rest of mankind that they can no more be examples for us. This is not so. Their life has been devoted to men, not only to redeem us by their achievement, but also to show us how we are to live in order to have a share in the Redemption. By choosing the Virgin-Mother Christ did not only prove that freely chosen and dedicated virginity is pleasing to God and has redemptive power; He has also said clearly that others, too, are called to virginity for the Kingdom of Heaven. We shall have to discuss later in how far this is a special vocation.

First it must be ascertained whether virginity is a specific form of feminine existence, so that it might be an end of feminine education. That this must be so seems to me proved by the fact that it has been proposed to us not only in Christ alone, but in Christ and Mary. In Christ God Himself confronts us. As the eternal Word is the image of the Father in which the Father contemplates Himself, so in the incarnate Word the image of the Father becomes visible to human eyes: "He who sees me sees the Father". The transcendence of the Lord over all creatures is revealed by the fact that the Man Christ is incapable of being tied to an individual creature. His humanity is entirely the instrument of His redemptive work, given Him to dispose of in personal freedom. His virginity is constitutive. This does not mean that He was not free to choose differently, but that there was no question of choosing. In this He is above all other men; everybody else has the possibility of choosing, just as no one can be united to God except by free choice. In this respect Mary's freely chosen virginity is the pattern to be followed by all, men and women alike. Her whole being is expressed in the words: "Behold the handmaid of the Lord". Her readiness to serve God excludes all other ties. It is true, the celibacy of priests is also based on the undivided service of the Lord. The difference lies in the way in which in either case the Lord transforms the readiness into actual service. He makes the priest His representative and again lets us see the Lord Himself in him. In Mary we do not see the Lord, but we see her always by His side. Her service is given immediately to Him; it is prayer interceding with Him for men, transmitting to them the grace she receives from His hands. She does not represent the Lord, but assists Him. In this her position is similar to that of Eve beside the first Adam. But she is placed there not for His sake, but for ours. She is the mother of the living not because they all originate from her in the course of the generations, but because her motherly love embraces the whole mystical Body together with its Head. In her virginity she is the pure type of all womanhood, because she stands beside Him who is the type of all manhood and leads all mankind to Him.

We may ask whether this womanhood that is serving love is a real image of the Godhead. Serving love means assistance that helps all creatures to lead them to perfection. Now this is the title that is given to the Holy Ghost. Thus we could see the primeval type of feminine being in the Spirit of God that is shed abroad over all creation. It finds its most perfect image in the purest Virgin, who is the bride of God and the Mother of all men; beside her are the virgins dedicated to God, who bear the title of honour 'Spouse of Christ' and are called to take part in the work of redemption. But her image are also those women who stand beside a man, who is Christ's image, and help to build up His body, the Church, through their motherhood which is both physical and spiritual.

If Mary is the prototype of pure womanhood, the imitation of Mary will have to be the end of feminine education. If the distribution of graces is entrusted to the hands of the Queen of Heaven, we shall aim not only at looking up to her, but also at trustfully uniting ourselves to her. This is not another way beside the imitation of Christ: the imitation of Mary includes the imitation of Christ, because Mary was His first follower and is the first and most perfect image of Christ. Therefore the imitation of Mary belongs not only to women, but to all Christians. But it is of special importance for women, because it will lead them to the feminine form of the image of Christ conformed to their nature.

While we were considering the order of Redemption, we found that there is no completely undifferentiated end for all women. Mary herself offers the most striking example, since, by choosing virginity, she separated herself from her people's traditional view of the vocation of woman. It is true, her vocation in the history of mankind was unique; yet in the course of time we repeatedly notice women who have a special definite purpose to fulfil. There are such even in the Old Testament, for example Judith and Esther, who are taken to be types of our Lady. Later, in the history of the Church, we have e.g. Catherine of Siena, Joan of Arc, the great St. Teresa, to name only those whose activities are removed from the ordinary ways of women in a particularly striking way. Yet such a special vocation is not a privilege restricted to a few chosen ones whose names are preserved in the annals of history. Every human soul is created by God, every one of them receives a character that distinguishes it from all others. This individuality is meant to be developed together with its humanity and femininity. It is called to an activity that corresponds to its innate personal qualities, the development of which has to be included in the aim of feminine education. It is impossible to give a picture of the individuality in the same way as the image of perfect humanity or perfect femininity can be outlined. But we must clearly understand that the aim is not wholly defined by these two, but that it can be fully achieved only in the concrete unity of an individual person. A flexible variety of educational ways and means are necessary to realize this, but beyond these we need especially confidence in one's own being and courage to be oneself. We must believe in our individual vocation to definite personal activity and be ready to listen to the call and to follow it. Thus we shall define the end of individual education as the formation of the person who is what she is personally meant to be, who goes her way and accomplishes the work given to her. This way will not be chosen arbitrarily; it is the way in which God leads her. If we would guide people toward the pure development of their individuality, we must teach them to trust in divine Providence and to be ready to read and follow the indications it gives them.

It is, indeed, impossible to give a notional presentation of the variety of individuality or to outline the individual educational end of every person; nevertheless, since we have been able to distinguish types, it is also possible to distinguish typical aims in the education of girls. While considering these types we shall have opportunities to discuss contemporary demands. First, however, we have to consider the fact that even when outlining the concept of pure womanhood we had to allow for differentiations.

The Virgin Mother was, on the one hand, the prototype of the Old Testament type of woman, who stands beside her husband, managing her household and bringing up her children in the fear of the Lord. On the other hand, she was also the type of the spouse of Christ, whose household is the kingdom of God, whose family is the Communion of Saints. We have first to ask ourselves whether, and in how far, this implies an either-or. If the Virgin Mother is the prototype of pure womanhood, both will in a certain sense have to be the end of all feminine education. For not only the dedicated virgin, but the whole Church and every Christian soul is called the spouse of Christ, since Mary is the pattern of the Church and of all Christians. Now, to be a spouse of Christ means to belong to the Lord and to prefer the love of Christ to everything else, not only from a theoretical conviction, but with all one's heart and in the practice of everyday life. It also means to be free from all creatures, from false attachments to oneself and others, for this is the most interior and spiritual sense of purity. A wife and mother, too, must possess this virginity of soul, indeed without it she will not be able to fulfil her task. For this spiritual virginity is the source of her serving love, which is neither slavery nor tyranny. On the other hand, the love of Christ will cause this serving love, which is the essence of motherliness, to overflow on to all creatures. Hence those women, who are not wives and mothers, will also have to exercize this spiritual motherliness, both in mind and action. Yet the fact that this ideal of the Virgin-Mother is binding on all women does not obliterate the difference of two types of women and two types of life. For it is no unimportant external whether or not a woman is also a wife and mother. It means that a human being grows into a larger psychosomatic organism. Body and soul must be specially suited to this process, and through being thus 'embodied' they will be formed in a special way. On the other hand, life outside marriage, too, requires a particular suitability of body and soul, and will in its turn produce a particular character. Thus we have here the parting of two ways which may be implicit in natural suitability. There are warm-hearted girls of strong vitality needing close human relationships, who will long to live in common, to look after others, and to have an outlet for their practical abilities. They would seem to have a natural aptitude for family life. For girls with less developed instincts and an inclination to recollection and solitude a celibate life seems more easily possible. However, natural suitability alone is not decisive; by itself it does not constitue perfect aptitude for either way. Marriage and family life do not only require full development, but also a large measure of self-restraint, and the pruning and transformation of natural vital and social instincts. Something similar holds good for the other way. Nevertheless, life does not always lead on to the way indicated by natural aptitude; the vocation may even be opposed to it. Thus, on the one hand, we have to include both ways in our education work, on the other it is very difficult to combine them.

This, in my opinion, is the central practical problem of feminine education; its solution is the Catholic answer to contemporary questions. It should be the fruit of an ideal, that is to say of a completely adequate education to make every girl ready for both, marriage and celibacy. This aim would be achieved on the one hand by physical strength and health, by untrammelled natural feeling, that is prepared for sacrifice and self-denial, on the other by overcoming the instincts through strengthening the spiritual side. Today we need more than ever mothers who correspond to the ideal of the valiant woman. And because we have to see the normal development in the vocation of physical motherhood, we should adapt the normal type of feminine education to this end. Nevertheless, since even those whose natural aptitude points to this are not at all certain that they will be able to achieve it, they should also be trained for the other way. Natural aptitude for celibacy is exceptional. Yet the vocation to be virgins consecrated to God is not given only to those with a natural disposition for it. Today many are called to remain unmarried whose nature and inclinations had seemed to destine them for the other way. Education must provide for all these cases, so that the call of God, which may be made as clear by external circumstances as by the inclination of the heart, should be accepted neither rebelliously nor resignedly, but with willing co-operation. If the call to the virginal life is received with joy, even though it may not include the religious state nor be in accordance with natural inclinations, there will be a strong probability that the feminine nature will not suffer harm. The basis for such an attitude is the mind of 'the handmaid of the Lord', which should be the aim and the fruit of religious education. Besides, all the powers and faculties must contribute to the fruitful development of nature.

If a girl belongs to the type that shows a natural aptitude for domestic work and motherhood, her education should aim at making her fit for a job adapted to these capacities. If the domestic abilities are more pronounced, she should be trained for domestic, agricultural and land work, perhaps also for business, in the other case for nursing, educational and social work. The more intellectual type should be trained for creative or subordinate intellectual work whether scholarly, artistic or concerned with organization. Thus we have specialization on a common foundation. This aim of professional efficiency must be kept in view in the interests of a sound development of the individual personality, but also because it meets the social demand for integrating the feminine contribution in the national and cultural life. Hence one of the aims of feminine education must be to provide instruction on the structure and laws of the state and of society, so that women may adapt their personal activities to the social whole, and also because they will be the more prepared to do this if they understand the social importance of their efforts.

By thus taking the eternal order as our guide, we are led to a consideration of all the demands we had met in the beginning: suitability for marriage and motherhood, professional efficiency, political and social responsibility, all of which rest on the desire to serve God. It is true, only those contemporary demands that result from our view of the contemporary scene can be harmonized with the eternal order. This same order demands with equal insistence that the demands of another *Weltanschauung* should be rejected. We have to reject a social order and a form of education which completely deny the special characteristics and destiny of woman, which refuse to admit an organic co-operation of the sexes as well as organic social entities, but would treat all individuals as so many cogs in a mechanically regulated economy. We shall also reject a social order and a system of education that value humanity and sexual relations merely biologically, failing to recognize the autonomy and superiority of the spiritual and intellectual in comparison with the vital forces, and knowing even less of a supernatural orientation. Today there is no other bulwark against these contemporary currents than the Catholic faith and a metaphysical, social and educational theory and practice that rest on this faith. By advocating an autonomous feminine education comprising all cultural spheres, we are defending not only the threatened position of woman in our civilization, but by doing so we are taking our place in the great struggle of the spirit against materialism and biologism, as fighters for the kingdom of Christ against all un-Christian and anti-Christian trends and movements.

C. THE ETHOS OF WOMEN'S PROFESSIONS

Is it possible to speak of a special profession of women or even of a multiplicity of professions? Radical feminist leaders, especially in the beginning of the movement, have denied the first question and claimed all professions for their sex. Their opponents will not admit the second; they recognize only one vocation, the 'natural' one. The subject requires a discussion of both points of view. We must first ask whether there is a natural vocation of woman, and what is the psychological attitude it requires.

Only pugnacious passion could blind a person to such an extent to make her deny the palpable fact that the body and soul of woman have been formed for a particular purpose. The clear, unshakable word of Scripture says what daily experience has taught from the beginning of the world: woman is destined to be the companion of man and the mother of men. For this her body is equipped, and her psychological make-up, too, conforms to it. It is again a fact of experience that a psychological peculiarity exists; it also follows from St. Thomas' principle that the soul is the form of the body. Where the bodies are so fundamentally different, there must also be a different type of soul, despite the common human nature. We would outline this typically feminine psychological attitude only quite briefly, since it is really quite familiar to all of us.

Woman tends towards the living and personal; she wants the whole. To cherish, to keep and protect, this is her natural, her authentically maternal desire. The dead thing, the 'object', interests her in the first place insofar as it serves the living and the personal rather than for its own sake. This is connected with another feature: every kind of abstraction is foreign to her nature. The living and personal which is the object of her care, is a concrete whole and must be cared for and encouraged as a whole, not one part at the expense of the others, not the mind at the expense of the body or *vice versa*, neither one faculty of the soul at the expense of the others. This she tolerates neither in herself nor in others. And to this practical attitude corresponds her theoretical endowment: her natural way of knowledge is not so much notional and analytical, but envisaging and sensing the concrete. This natural equipment enables a woman to nurse and bring up her own children; but this fundamental attitude is not confined to them; it is also her way of meeting her husband and all those who come near her.

This maternal character is matched by her gift of companionship. To share in another's life, to take part in all that concerns him, in the greatest as well as in the smallest things, in joy and in sorrow, but also in his work and problems, this is her special gift and her happiness. Man is absorbed in 'his cause' and expects others to be interested in, and ready to serve it. He normally finds it difficult to enter into the personalities and interests of others. But this is natural to woman, and she is able sympathetically to penetrate into spheres which are in themselves foreign to her, and for which she would never care if a personal interest did not attract her to them. This gift is closely connected with her maternal vocation. If a person takes a lively interest in another, the latter's capacities and performance will be increased. It is a truly maternal function even, and especially, needed by mature people; it will be given also to one's own children the more they grow up, replacing the lower functions.

Participation in the life of her husband requires submission and obedience, as they are enjoined by the Word of God. It is man's nature to serve his cause directly, whereas woman serves it for his sake, and so it is fit that she should do so under his guidance. It is true, the duty of obedience extends beyond this also to the direct domain of woman, to the household and the education of the children; but this is due perhaps not so much to the feminine peculiarity as to the 'natural vocation' of man as the head and protector of woman. The natural feminine inclination to obedience and service corresponds to this natural vocation. This presentation of the natural feminine character did not at first include an evaluation. It is immediately evident that, developed in its purity, it has a great vital value. But for this, as well as for its ethical value which has to be considered apart, it is essential that the feminine nature should be developed in its purity. Now this is by no means normal, we may even say that it will be so only in quite particular circumstances. For the feminine nature is as much stained by original sin as human nature in general, and thus hindered in its pure development. Unless its evil tendencies are opposed, they will lead to typical perversions. The personal tendency is usually unwholesomely exaggerated; on the one hand woman is inclined to be extravagantly concerned with her own person and to expect the same interest from others; this expresses itself in vanity, desire for praise and recognition and an unrestrained urge for self-expression and communication. On the other hand we shall find an unmeasured interest in others which shows itself as curiosity, gossip, and an indiscreet longing to penetrate into the intimate lives of other people. The tendency towards wholeness easily leads her to frittering away her energy, it makes her disinclined to discipline her individual talents properly and leads to superficial nibbling in all directions. In her attitude to others it shows itself in a possessiveness far exceeding what is required by her maternal functions. Thus the sympathetic companion becomes the interfering busybody that cannot tolerate silent growth and thus does not foster development, but hinders it. Thus joyful service has been replaced by lust for governing. Only too many unhappy marriages have been caused by this aberration, by which many mothers have also estranged their grown-up or even their growing children.

If, by way of contrast, we would paint the picture of the purely developed feminine nature, of the wife and mother as her natural destiny would have her be, we shall look to the immaculate Virgin. Her life is centred in her Son. She waits for Him to be born in blissful expectancy, she protects His childhood, she follows Him in His ways, whether closely or from a distance, according to His wishes. She holds His dead body in her arms and carries out His last will. But all this she does not according to her own liking. She is the handmaid of the Lord, who fulfils the task to which God has called her. Therefore she does not treat her Child as her property: she has received Him from the hand of God, and she places Him again back into His hand, offering Him in the temple and accompanying Him to His death on the Cross.

If we consider the Mother of God as a wife we shall be struck by her silent, limitless trust that counts on the same limitless confidence, and faithfully shares the other's sorrow. In everything she is subject to God's will that has given her her husband as her human protector and visible head.

In the image of the Mother of God we see the fundamental attitude of soul that corresponds to the natural vocation of woman. She is obedient to her husband, trusts him and takes part in his life, furthering his objective tasks as well as the development of his personality. She faithfully nurses and cherishes her Child, developing His God-given talents. She treats both with selfless devotion, silently retiring into the background when she is not needed. All this is based on the conception of marriage and motherhood as a vocation that comes from God, and must therefore be fulfilled for God's sake and under His guidance. How is it possible for a woman to reach such moral heights in mind as well as in deed, seeing that in her fallen nature such powerful instincts oppose this end and urge her on to other ways? A good natural remedy for all typically feminine weaknesses is thorough objective work. This demands in itself the repression of exaggerated personal interests; besides, it combats superficiality not only in one's own sphere of work, but provokes a general aversion against this failing. It requires submission to objective laws, hence it is a good training in obedience. But it must not lead to the sacrifice of the pure and praiseworthy personal attitude and to onesided specialization and enslavement by one's particular subject, which is the typical perversion of the masculine nature. This natural remedy is very effective, as is shown by the maturity and harmony of many women of high intellectual culture, and of others who have been trained in the discipline of strenuous professional work through the circumstances of their life. In this we have a parallel to the picture of the perfect gentleman which Newman once outlined in his *Idea of a University,* involving a culture of the personality which might easily be mistaken for sanctity. But in both cases this is only a matter of similarity. If a nature has been disciplined merely through education it will preserve its cultivated exterior only up to a point; if it is subjected to too strong a pressure it will break the barriers. Only the power of grace can transform the fallen nature not only from outside, but completely deracinate and re-form it from within. We shall discuss later how this happens in the case of the feminine nature.

We now approach the second main question: are there women's professions other than the natural one? Only prejudiced blindness could deny that women are capable of filling other professions than that of wife and mother. The experience of the last decades, and really the experience of all times has proved this. We may well say that in case of need every normal, healthy woman can do a job. And, conversely, there is no profession that could not be practised by a woman. If fatherless children have to be provided with a breadwinner, if orphaned brothers and sisters or old parents have to be supported, a woman ready to make sacrifices can achieve the most astonishing things. But individual gifts and inclinations, too, may lead to the most varied activities. Indeed, no woman is only 'woman'; every one has her individual gifts just as well as a man, and so is capable of professional work of one sort or another, whether it be artistic, scholarly, technical or any other. Theoretically this individual talent may extend to any sphere, even to those somewhat outside women's scope. In such a case we would not speak of a 'feminine profession'. For this term can only apply to professions whose work depends on the special feminine gifts, that is all those concerned with nursing, education, social work and sympathetic understanding. Such are the professions of the doctor and the nurse, of the teacher and the governess, of the domestic servant as well as the whole range of those devoted to modern social work. In the sphere of scholarship those sciences that are concerned with the concrete and the personal will be most suited to women, as also anything that tends to assist others, such as translating and editing, and perhaps the sympathetic guidance of the work of others.

It is evident that all this sort of work needs basically the same psychological attitude as that of the wife and mother; but it extends to a wider sphere and mostly to a changing circle of people, hence it is largely detached from the vital blood relationship and elevated to a more spiritual sphere. But for this reason it also lacks the force of the natural instincts latent in the community of life, and needs a greater capacity for sacrifice.

Over and above this, however, we may say that also professions whose strictly objective requirements do not suit the feminine nature and could rather be considered as specifically masculine, may yet be practised in a genuinely feminine way. We are thinking of work in a factory, in a business office, in national or municipal administration, in legislation, in a chemical laboratory or in a mathematical institute. All this needs concentration on things devoid of life, or is concerned with abstract thought. Yet in the great majority of cases the work will involve being together with others at least in the same room, often also in division of labour. And with this we have at once an opportunity for developing all the feminine virtues. One may even say that precisely here, where everyone is in danger of becoming a piece of the machine, the development of the specifically feminine can become a beneficial counter-influence. In the soul of a man who knows that help and sympathy are awaiting him at his place of work, much will be kept alive or aroused that would otherwise be dwarfed. This is one way of feminine individuality forming professional life in a mode different from the average man's.

Another way is also possible. Every abstract thing is ultimately part of a concrete. All that is dead ultimately serves the living. Therefore every abstract activity ultimately serves a living whole. If we are capable of obtaining and preserving this view of the whole, it will remain with us however dull and abstract our work, which will then become tolerable and in many cases be performed much better and more adequately than if preoccupation with the parts made us forget the whole. When working out laws and decrees a man might perhaps aim at the most perfect legal form, with little regard to concrete situations; whereas a woman who remains faithful to her nature even in parliament or in the administrative services, will keep the concrete end in view and adapt the means accordingly.

Thus is might be a blessing for the whole social life whether private or public, if women penetrated increasingly into the most different professional spheres, especially if they preserve the specifically feminine ethos. Here again the Mother of God should be our example. Mary at the wedding of Cana: her quietly observing eyes see everything and discover where something is missing. And before anyone notices anything, before there is any embarrassment, she has already remedied the situation. She finds ways and means, she gives the necessary directions, everything quietly and without attracting attention. Let this be the example of woman in the professional life. Wherever she is placed, let her do her work quietly and efficiently, without demanding attention or recognition. And at the same time she should keep a vigilant eye on the situation, sensing where there is something lacking, where somebody needs her help, and rectifying things as far as possible without being noticed. Then, like a good angel, she will always spread blessing.

We have now surveyed the sphere of feminine activities in the domestic as well as in public life, indeed, a rich and fertile field. Yet this does not exhaust her capacities. Today as at all times since the foundation of Christ's Church the Lord has called His chosen ones from their families and professions to His own service. Can the religious vocation be regarded as a specially feminine one? Both men and women receive this call, which is supernatural. For it comes from above and asks a person to rise above the natural earthly sphere. And thus it looks as if here the natural differences might carry no weight. Yet there is the theological principle that grace does not destroy, but that it perfects nature. Thus we may expect that in the religious vocation, too, the feminine nature will not be eliminated, but will be integrated and made fruitful in a special way. Beyond this it is possible that, like the natural professions, the religious life, too, may make special demands that appeal to the feminine nature in a special way. The religious vocation implies the complete surrender of the whole human being and of its whole life to the service of God. Religious are bound to use all the means suited to promote this end, such as renunciation of property, of vital human ties and of their own will. This may be achieved in many forms, that is to say the Lord may call His own to serve Him in many different ways. They may silently contemplate the divine truth or solemnly celebrate the liturgy; they may spread the faith by the apostolate, or devote themselves to works of mercy. Thus the religious body consists of many different members. If we examine the various activities of religious, and how they are apportioned to the sexes, we shall find that they are differently related to them according to their differences. We may safely consider contemplation and liturgical prayer as transcending the difference of sex, since they are truly angelic activities. The spreading of the faith, since it is included in the priestly vocation to teach, is predominantly the task of men, though women, too, are active in this sphere, especially in the teaching Orders. Works of charity, on the other hand, and the sacrificial life of atoning satisfaction, appeal quite definitely to the feminine nature. In the older Orders which have men's and women's branches, the work is normally divided in such a way that the men are engaged in the outside activities such as preaching and giving missions, whereas the women devote themselves to the silent apostolate of prayer and sacrifice, although the education of the young was added to their tasks at an early age. The active women's Congregations of modern times are generally engaged in thoroughly feminine activities in the fields of education and charitable work. Thus today, when the majority of feminine communities devote themselves to external activities, the work of the religious Sisters is materially scarcely different from that of the women 'in the world'. The only difference is the 'formal' one, that in the religious life all is done under obedience and for the love of God.

We would now examine how this formal element of the religious life is related to the nature of woman. The motive, principle and end of the religious life is complete surrender to God in self-forgetting love. The religious puts an end, as it were, to his own life, in order to make room for the life of God. The more completely this is realized, the richer will be the divine life that fills the soul. Now the divine life is an overflowing love that needs nothing for itself, but gives itself freely, mercifully condescending to every needy creature. It is a love that heals the sick and restores to life what is dead, that protects and fosters, nourishes, teaches and forms. It mourns with the mourning and rejoices with the joyful; it makes itself the servant of every being, so that it may become what the Father has destined it to be; in one word: it is the love of the divine Heart.

It is the deepest desire of a woman's heart to surrender itself lovingly to another, to be wholly his and to possess him wholly. This is at the root of her tendency towards the personal and the whole, which seems to us the specifically feminine characteristic. Where this total surrender is made to a human being, it is a perverted self-surrender that enslaves her, and implies at the same time an unjustified demand which no human being can fulfil. Only God can receive the complete surrender of a person, and in such a way that she will not lose, but gain her soul. And only God can give Himself to a human being in such a way that He will fulfil its whole being while losing nothing of His own. Hence the total surrender which is the principle of the religious life, is at the same time the only possible adequate fulfilment of woman's desire.

Now the divine love that enters the heart which is surrendered to God is a merciful love that would serve, awaken and foster life. It completely corresponds to what we have affirmed to be the professional ethos demanded of woman.

What practical consequence follows from this? It certainly does not follow that all women who would fulfil their vocation should become nuns. But it does follow that the fallen and perverted feminine nature can be restored to its purity and led to the heights of the vocational ethos such as the pure feminine nature represents, only if it is totally surrendered to God. Whether she lives as a mother in her home, in the limelight of public life or behind the silent walls of a convent, she must everywhere be a 'handmaid of the Lord', as the Mother of God had been in all the circumstances of her life, whether she was living as a virgin in the sacred precincts of the Temple, silently kept house at Bethlehem and Nazareth, or guided the apostles and the first Christian community after the death of her Son. If every woman were an image of the Mother of God, a spouse of Christ and an apostle of the divine Heart, she would fulfil her feminine vocation no matter in what circumstances she lived and what her external activities might be.

If I were to end here, the demands I have outlined, which are so frighteningly different from the average life of the present-day women, might seem the dreams of a starry-eyed idealist. I must therefore add a few words on how they can be carried out in practice. We will therefore calmly face the contrast between the average life of modern women and our demands. Many of the best are almost crushed by the double burden of professional and family duties; they are always busy, worn out, nervy and irritable. Where are they to find the interior calm and serenity in order to be a support and guide for others? In consequence there are daily little frictions with husband and children despite real mutual love and recognition of the other's merits, hence unpleasantness in the home and the loosening of family ties. In addition, there are the many superficial and unstable women who want only amusement in order to fill the interior void, who marry and are divorced, and leave their children either to themselves or to servants no more conscientious than the mothers. If they have to take a job they regard it only as a means to earn their living and to get as much enjoyment out of life as possible. In their case one can talk neither of vocation nor of ethos. They are like dry leaves blown by the wind. The breaking up of the family and the decline of morals is essentially connected with this group and can only be stemmed if we succeed in diminishing its number through suitable educational methods. Finally we would consider the by no means negligible number of those who take up a profession that corresponds to their talents and inclination. Nevertheless, many of them will discover after their first enthusiasm is spent that their expectations have not been fulfilled, and will be longing for something else. This may often be due to the fact that they were trying to do their work 'just like a man'. They have not sought—or perhaps not found—the means to make their feminine characteristics fruitful in their professional work. Then the nature that has been denied and repressed will assert itself.

If we look behind the walls of convents we shall find that even there the average nun does not realize the ideal in its fullness. It is true, at all times there have been religious who did not take in the full meaning of their vows, or who were ready for the complete sacrifice in the first enthusiasm of youth, but could not keep it up. They will usually be a torment to themselves and a burden to their community. Add to this the difficulties produced by modern circumstances: there is, for example, the twofold burden of the nun who has to keep up to the standard of the contemporary demands made on a nurse, a teacher or a social worker, while at the same time fulfilling the obligations of her religious life. Only too often she will lose the right attitude under this twofold strain, in the same way as the wife and mother who has a job.

Yet, despite this sad picture of the average, true heroines may still be met in all spheres of life, working real miracles of love and achievement in their families and professions, as well as in the cloister. We all know them from the records of the Church, but also from our own experience; there are the mothers who radiate warmth and light in their homes, who bring up nine children of their own, showering blessings on them for their own lives as well as for coming generations, and who still have a large heart for the needs of others. There are the teachers and office staff who support a whole family out of their salary, do domestic chores before and after their professional work, and still have time and money for all sorts of Church and charitable activities. There are the nuns who spend their nights praying for souls in danger, and take up voluntary penances for sinners. Where do they all find the strength to perform tasks which one might often think impossible for nature, and yet preserve that unalterable peace and serenity despite the most exacting nervous and emotional strains?

Only by the power of grace can nature be purged from its

dross, restored to its purity and made ready to receive the divine life. And this life itself is the fountain from which spring the works of love. If we want to preserve it, we must nourish it constantly from the source whence it flows unceasingly, that is from the holy Sacraments, above all from the Sacrament of Love. A woman's life for which the divine love is to be its inner form, will have to be a eucharistic life. To forget oneself, to be delivered from all one's own desires and pretensions, to open one's heart to all the pressing needs of others—this is possible only through the daily intimacy with our Lord in the tabernacle. If we visit the eucharistic God and take counsel with Him in all our affairs, if we let ourselves be purified by the sanctifying power that flows from the altar of sacrifice, if we offer ourselves to the Lord in this sacrifice and receive Him into our inmost souls in Holy Communion, then we cannot but be drawn ever more deeply into the current of this divine life; we shall grow into the mystical Body of Christ, and our heart will be transformed into the likeness of the divine Heart.

Something else is closely connected with this. If we have entrusted all the cares of our earthly life to the divine Heart, our own heart will have been freed from them, and our soul will be ready to share in the divine life. We shall walk by the side of the Redeemer in the same way that He walked when He was on earth, and in which He still continues in His mystical life. With the eyes of faith we shall penetrate even into the secret life within the Godhead. Moreover, this participation in the divine life has a liberating power; it lightens the weight of our earthly concerns and gives us even in this temporal life a glimpse of eternity, a reflexion of the life of the blessed, by which we walk in the light. How we can thus walk, as it were hand in hand with God, He has shown us Himself through the liturgy of the Church. Therefore the life of a truly Catholic woman will be guided by the liturgy. If we pray with the Church in spirit and in truth, our whole life will be formed by this prayer.

Summing up we would say: every profession that satisfies the feminine soul and is capable of being formed by it is a genuine feminine profession. The inmost formative principle of the feminine soul is the love that springs from the divine Heart. A woman will live by this principle if she closely joins herself to the divine Heart in a eucharistic and liturgical life.

PHILOSOPHICAL WRITINGS

From CONTRIBUTIONS TO A PHILOSOPHICAL FOUNDATION OF PSYCHOLOGY

1. Motivation as a Fundamental Law of the Life of the Mind.

Leaving the abstract sphere in which the discussion has to far moved, we now consider a new circle of phenomena. The ego has until now been living in the stream (i.e. of consciousness) within the sequence of those data it 'had' without 'looking at' them. Now it opens its intellectual eye and directs itself towards something; something confronts it and becomes an 'object' for it. A lower form of intentionality, correlative to objectivity, is already included in having the immanent data. The fact that we are directing ourselves towards something we now have in mind, i.e. the intention that arises on the ground of the immanent data, signifies a new class of experiences of units, constituting themselves in the stream. It is the class of views or apprehensions *(Auffassungen)* or acts, here taken in the widest sense of intentional experience, not of a specific deed. They are the beginning of the mind's life. The glance of the ego may here take different directions: it can be a looking back on the experience that has just passed (whether it still has vital repercussions or is already concluded) no matter whether it was a sensation or an act. In this case we have a reflexion. The glance need not, however, be directed to a datum or sensation, but may penetrate through it to something that no longer belongs to the stream itself, but is related to the individual consciousness only through this glance of the ego and its position in the stream, that is it may be directed toward an external object, something transcending the stream. The place of the sensible datum *(Empfindungsdatum)* is taken by an 'image one has in mind', a coloured shape or a sound 'outside me' (no matter what kind of space is meant by this outside). In the realm of acts there are now new modes of interrelation which we have not yet met. If the glance be directed consecutively to a number of data continually following each other, or rather through these to 'external' objectivities *(Gegenständlichkeiten)* we have not only a disconnected series of separate conceptions of individual images, but one continuous conception that adds what comes later to what came before (apperception), a grouping together of individual conceptions (synthesis) and a 'being moved' of the latter by the former (motivation). All this has a meaning only in the sphere of the acts of an ego, for in the sphere of pure passivity with which we have been concerned before (i.e. in the preceding chapters, not in this anthology. Ed.) there can be no question of taking, grasping or moving.

If we call the connexion of acts such as here envisaged generally 'motivation', we are conscious of departing from the usual terminology, which confines this term to the sphere of 'free acts', especially of the will. We believe, however, that this wider usage is fully justified. For we have here in view a general structure applicable to the whole sphere of intentional experiences, which is differently shaped only according to the peculiarity of the acts that fall within its scope. What is ordinarily called motivation should also prove to be such a special form.

Motivation in our general sense is that connexion into which acts as such enter with one another. It is no mere blending as that of the phases of the flux of experiences occurring simultaneously or one after the other, nor the association of experiences, but a proceeding from one another, one shaping itself or being shaped by reason, and for the sake, of the other. The structure of those experiences that alone can enter the relation of motivation is absolutely essential to the nature of this relationship. It is this, that acts originate in the pure ego, arising from it phenomenally, and aiming at something objective. The point of departure of this motivation will always be the ego. It performs one act because it has performed the other. Here the 'performance' need not yet be taken in the sense of a genuine spontaneity. It is characteristic of the relationship of motivation that it can appear in different forms; it may be explicitly performed, but it may also be there implicitly. We have e.g. the case of an explicit motivation if we proceed in the context of a syllogism from the premises to the conclusion, understanding and believing the latter on the basis of the premises. If, on the other hand, we conduct a mathematical proof, using a theorem which we have earlier understood because of its suppositions, but which we are now not going to prove again, then belief in this theorem is a motivated belief, though the motivation has not been actually carried out, but is implicit in the concrete act, by which the theorem is in our mind as a unity and in the certain form of belief. Essentially every explicit motivation, once it has been accomplished, passes over into an implicit one, and essentially every implicit motivation, e.g. the one contained in the belief in a thesis that has not yet been proved but has been 'intuitively' anticipated, can be explicated. In the various spheres of intentional experience now the one and now the other form of motivation will predominate. In the sphere of simple perception we are generally concerned with implicit motivation.

In the first place, the conception of a thing as such has already been elicited by a certain course the sense data have taken. This eliciting we may call a lower form of motivation, much the same as the fact that we have sensations is a lower form of intentionality. Within this concept the real relations of motivation make their appearance: because I apprehend an object that extends in space, I also perceive 'with it' its back, which I do not apprehend itself, and this co-perception in its turn perhaps motivates a free movement, which allows the back that has been 'co-perceived' with the object to be actually perceived. We can also take the special way an object is 'given' as a motive for the attitude of the ego to this object, e.g. the fact that it is perceived may be the motive for believing in its existence. Here, too, we have an intentional experience, which radiates from the ego to the object and is, in this sense, 'performed' by it, without being a free action of the ego. Belief in its existence can in its turn be the motive for asserting this existence in a judgement, with which we already enter the sphere of genuine spontaneity. Moreover, belief in the existence of a certain fact can motivate belief in the existence of another. Grasping a value can motivate an emotional attitude (e.g. delight in beauty), and possibly a willing and acting (e.g. carrying out an action that has been recognized as morally right). All these acts are very different, yet they have one common characteristic: the ego effects one experience—or it is given to the ego—*because* it has another, for the sake of another. As has been said, this common structural feature is not changed by the fact that in some cases the motivating experience is clearly distinguished from the motivated one as independent acts following each other (as e.g. premise and conclusion, or perception of a value and act of the will) while in others they unite to the oneness of a concrete act (as self-apprehension and belief in the perception). Here we have always taken that experience as motivating, by reason of which the other takes place, the latter for the motivated one, with the ego in the rôle of the mediator. But to understand motivation it is also necessary to consider the correlates of experience. The relation between act and motivation may be elucidated by the following consideration: wherever consciousness is directed towards an object, it does not take it as an empty x, but with a certain content of meaning: it apprehends it as bearing a unified 'stock of being' *(Seinsbestand)* of which, however, only a part comes into full view and is perfectly realized, while all else is only vaguely 'also meant' by it. This applies in the first place to the perception of, say, a thing perceived as a body in space, only part of whose surface is actually presented to view. But it also applies e.g. to the understanding of a sentence or a factual relationship *(Sachverhalt)* which have from the first been intended as a whole, but are actually grasped only gradually. The unity of sense lays down which supplements are admitted by a given partial sense, and which further steps can therefore be motivated by the first step. While living in the performance of an act, the ego is turned towards the object and envisages it, progressing from one act to another, with a constantly changing stock of meaning—changing, that is with regard to the relation of partial meanings which are given both full and empty—without being turned to the meaning itself and the combinations of motivations. But it is always possible to take the meaning as one's object, to analyze it and derive from *it* what norms are required for the course of motivation. It belongs e.g. to the meaning of two given statements that they are capable of entering into the unity of a syllogism by having a third as their consequence. Hence we derive the demand that every one who has pronounced these two judgements as premises should derive also the conclusion that follows from them. It belongs to the meaning of something that has been recognized as valuable that it presents itself at the same time as something that ought to be. From this must be derived the norm that if a person is concerned with a value (together with its non-existence and the possibility of realizing it) he should aim at its realization. Thus it is understandable that the whole life of the acts is subject to laws of reason which make the subject intelligible to itself, and by which it can measure the actual course of its motivation.

Viewed from this angle, the actually motivating factor in the course of a motivation does not seem to be the performance of the initial act, but the content of meaning of this act; and for this we will retain the customary term of motive. Lightning itself becomes for me the motive for expecting the thunderclap, not the perception of lightning; the arrival of the desired letter is the motive of my joy, not the realization of its arrival. But in as much as the motives can be motives only as correlates of such acts (not as something that exists objectively), the acts, too, participate in the origins of motivation. We may call them motivants, as distinct from motives, and the motivated acts motivates. In order to estimate the relations between motivation and the laws of reason correctly, we have to add some complementary details. First, the demands made by the sense-contents of an act are not always univocal. A fact may enter the most varied logical contexts and admit of a corresponding number of conclusions. Nevertheless, it limits a sphere of possibilities, and if the knowing subject goes beyond this sphere, it acts unreasonably. In the same way a value may limit the sphere of various possible attitudes of the subject accepting it. Now it is possible that the contents of an experience do not demand one definite motivate, but one of the various possible ones. There is yet another possibility: an experienced motive may admit certain ways of behaviour without demanding any of them. Here, too, there is still a meaningful connexion between motive and motivate, when one can be understood through the other, but there is no longer the relation of logical causation. It is quite understandable that a noise near me should attract my attention, or that I should instinctively tend to be in surroundings I like, but it is neither reasonable nor unreasonable. But if, on the other hand, I sought the society of people who are repellent to me, and precisely for this reason that they are repellent, this would not only be unreasonable but 'mad'.

Where the experienced motivation rests on a relation of reasonable causation, we shall speak of 'motives of reason'; where, on the other hand, there is only an understandable connexion, we can also call the motive stimulus.

Owing to the motivation that mediates the transitions from one act to the other, there grow in the stream of experience complexes of acts and motivations, which are constituted units analogous to the lasting experiences, such as sense data, that have been discussed above. Nevertheless, there are differences. An act always means leaving the stream; it grows out of the stream, but it is not absorbed in it; it 'grasps' something that does not belong to the course of the stream, it continues to generate itself as long as it clings to the object, and ceases when it lets it go. Hence we have no continuum of acts in the stream, no perpetual flowing into each other of acts, no perpetually filled 'field of acts' analogous to the fields of sense. The acts are 'sections', 'incisions' in the stream (the continuity of which is yet not broken by them, owing to the other constantly filled fields of experience) and it is possible that consciousness can flow on over stretches with no acts occurring in it. But since motivation causes one act to emerge from the other in the consciousness, the above-mentioned units grow into a new kind of 'complexes' which as such alternately sink into the stream and emerge from it. Unified objects correspond to these act-complexes as correlates that are inseperable from them. As the apprehensions, so also that which is apprehended unites into an objective entity. The unity of the object corresponds to the unity of a perception, and if a perception revives (i.e. if I remember something), the object presents itself before my eyes as a whole, not a side-view of it, as an isolated image. Hence what we have said in an earlier chapter on 'contact association' also extends to the sphere of intentional experiences, to the acts as well as to their correlates. But apprehension and motivation are presupposed if such an 'associative unity' is to arise; they are not, conversely, to be derived from it, as the sensualist psychology of association would have it.

After what has been said, the association according to causality seems no longer a problem. As the teaching on the constitution of objects shows, the perception of an object includes the apprehension of the causal connexions in which it is implicated, and the causal event itself constitutes itself in the consciousness as an harmonious objectivity, within which cause and effect are to be distinguished. Owing to this unified apprehension the one is given with, or aroused by, the other. But here, as in the case of the 'similarity association', this is not the only possible interpretation. It is true, the similarity of two given objects and these objects *as* similar enter into one unified perception, to that we can understand if, in future, 'one reminds us of the other'. But it is not immediately evident from the contact why an object should also remind us of another without either both, or their similarity (or other relationship) having been given together before. This needs to be specially elucidated.

As we have seen, the sphere of 'meaning' and of 'reason' begins with the acts and their motivations. We have here 'rightness' and 'wrongness', intelligibility and its reverse in a sense not to be found in the sphere of 'act-less' consciousness. I may, indeed, 'understand' it to be a natural necessity that the whole course of experience is influenced by the change of emotional states *(Lebensgefuehl)*, but the change in the one is not *caused* by the other, as is the case in motivation. In the one sphere we have the blind happenings, in the other a 'seeing' action or at least, in the case of implicit motivation, a happening that can be translated into a 'seeing' action. Understanding in the one sphere grasps the necessity of the event, in the other it repeats the originally accomplished seeing.

This needs some further elucidation. What has been said about the character of motivation will be admitted without difficulty if we refer it to the sphere of the specifically logical acts, where the syllogistic method proceeds from premises to conclusions. It is also immediately evident in the practical sphere, where a feeling produces a decision of the will, and a decision leads to an action. Here we have a 'logical consequence' and an 'intelligible process', this is evident. But what happens in the case from which we started, following the gradation of its constitution? A simple perception is neither a syllogistic process nor an action of the will (although there are philosophical systems that present it as such). And yet what we have said about it remains correct, and we find in all the cases that have been discussed a formal identity of the structure of experience. The only difference is that in the higher grades of the exercize of acts we experience motivation in a special sense by living 'in' it and 'consciously' exercizing it, so that it is immediately obvious to reflexion. In the lower grades, on the other hand, we have a 'hidden' activity of reason, the motivations take place 'in the dark' and have to be brought to light by careful reflective analysis. In such an analytical procedure the process of perception can be brought out of its darkness and, as it were, repeated in daylight in all its stages. Let no one say that this would mean studying a new experience in the place of ordinary perception. For the repetition is meant to be precisely a repetition of the experience such as it has originally taken place. The repetition is an intelligible process, in which each step is taken explicitly, and based on the preceding one. And precisely for this reason the original course of the experience also appears as one that might be accomplished intelligibly. On the other hand, it would be a completely senseless attempt if we would 'repeat' the causally conditioned changes of the stream of experience themselves, such as the motivation or the progress from one act to the other. In this sphere things can neither be 'executed' nor 'repeated'. Hence there is a radical difference between causality and motivation which can neither be bridged nor softened. This is expressed also in the fact that causality has its equivalent in the sphere of physical nature, whereas motivation has not.

2. *Motivation in the Sphere of Cognizance* (Kenntnisnahme); *the 'Inclination' (turning towards:* Zuwendung).

After defining the homogeneous character of motivation from without, we will now try to work out the special features it admits by considering the various kind of intentional experience that can enter into the context of motivation.

We would first consider the 'cognizance' of objects, the perception of a thing, the grasping of the facts of a case *(Sachverhalt)* etc. Here we have on the one hand a simple acceptance, which itself has no motive on the same level of consciousness, but only in the substrata of sense, but which (or the sense-contents of which) can in its turn become a motive for a further acceptance. Here the ego does nothing that it may not also leave undone, but it knows one thing because it has known another. But there are other acts connected with this acceptance of what is received, which are left to the good pleasure of the ego. These are the fact that I am 'turning towards' the object of which I already have a certain knowledge, and my progress towards further data. I must have 'taken in' something in order to be able to 'turn towards' it. What has been received in the quite definite manner which it possessed before the ego turned towards it, serves as a motive, or better as a stimulus, for turning towards it. It exercizes an attraction on the ego which this may either follow or refuse. The 'freedom' of 'turning towards' consists in this twofold possibility, it does not signify a total lack of motive.

3. *Attitudes* (Stellungnahmen), *their Acceptance and Rejection.*

The facts of taking cognizance or their correlates may further motivate a new species of experiences, the 'attitudes' or positions that are to be taken up. If I perceive a thing I begin to believe in its existence; if I recognize a fact I come to be convinced of its being so; if I perceive admirable qualities in a person I shall begin to admire him. Taking up an attitude, as taking cognizance, is something that is 'given' to me. I cannot take up attitudes or positions as if I were freely turning towards something. I cannot decide for or against them arbitrarily. This is so for two reasons: (1) The attitude is *due* to the object to which it is given, the object demands it. It is not only called forth, but *caused* by it. If I were to decide against it, I should by doing so act in opposition to reasonable norms (which is not normally the case if one refuses to turn towards a thing). (2) The attitudes do not as a rule offer themselves (like the inclinations) before they appear, but they are simply there as soon as we take cognizance of a thing, without leaving us any choice. They take possession of me; on the other hand, I cannot procure them if they fail to appear on their own account. I may for example long for religious faith; I may strive for it with all my might, yet it need not come to me. I may occupy myself with a great character without being able to admire it as it deserves. Hence I am not free in this respect. On the other hand, there is a possibility which does not exist if I merely take cognizance of a thing: I can take up an attitude to the attitudes in a new sense; I can accept them, agree with or refuse them. I accept them: that is I gladly surrender to them without resistance if they arise in me. Or I may refuse them; but this does not mean that I do away with them. This is not in my power. In order to 'cross out' a belief I need new motives by which the motives of the original belief are annulled, and which result quite normally in eliminating this belief. But I need not admit this belief; I may behave as if it did not exist. I may render it ineffective. Husserl calls this attitude *epoché*. I may e.g. expect news that will necessitate a journey. I then hear from non-authoritative quarters that the expected event has happened. I believe it at once; yet I do not 'want to' believe it as long as I have no authentic information. I behave as I should if I did not believe it: I make no preparations, I continue to go about my daily business, though the attitude of believing undoubtedly exists. We will give an example to show that not only certain actions (hence even 'free' acts) are omitted, but that the *epoché* can actually render the existing attitude ineffective, so that even the attitudes that are not free fail to appear.

A mother hears from his comrades that her son has been killed. She is convinced that he is dead, but she does not 'want' to believe it as long as she has no official confirmation. Now as long as she refuses to assent to her belief, she does not feel any sorrow, which is at once aroused when she believes in his death without anything to prevent this belief. (This fact that sorrow is prevented if the motivating belief is neutralized differs, of course, fundamentally from fighting the sorrow when it arises). Another example. A convinced atheist realizes the existence of God in a religious experience. He cannot avoid belief, but he does not assent to it; he does not allow it to take effect, but remains undauntedly attached to his scientific view of the world, which would be completely upset by unqualified faith. Or, finally: a person arouses my affection without my being able to prevent it; but I will not admit it interiorly and avoid it. This, too, is quite different from fighting an affection to which one does not want to surrender. As long as the interior assent was withheld, the struggle would have no meaning at all. If the affection is rendered ineffective in this way, I omit not only those actions that would have to motivate it, but even the involuntary expressions of a genuine affection will fail to appear; they simply do not occur. This acceptance or refusal of an attitude, to which it owes the character of its full vitality and efficacy or, on the other hand, of its neutrality, need not be independently performed acts, the attitude may appear at once as invested with either character. Yet these acts, too, may be freely performed at any time. How truly 'free' I feel in performing them is proved by this, that I am conscious not only of thus actually bringing the belief to life, but, as it were, of giving existence to the very fact I believe. By according unhindered belief to the news of death I feel as if I myself made it irrevocable only by my assent. As long as I refuse this assent, I feel as if I were still holding up fate. The counterpart of this refusal of an existing attitude is the acceptance of one that does not exist.

I can assume a belief which I do not in fact have, which is not alive in me. For example, I assume that I am sufficiently certain of the circumstances of my life to be able to make plans. I decide, let us say, to make a journey next year, to move into another town, to finish a work I have begun etc., and I organize my life completely in accordance with these future plans. Nevertheless, I am in fact firmly convinced that some event will upset all my plans. But I refuse to assent to this living belief and do not let it become effective in me. The refusal of an attitude is always equivalent to the taking up of an opposite one, which now governs my further behaviour, although it is not a genuine, living attitude.

Taking up and refusal of attitudes have their motives and their causes just as much as the attitudes themselves. Motive and cause may be identical (as in the cases just mentioned), but they may also differ. I refuse, for example, to believe the news because the person who announces it is untrustworthy. His untrustworthiness, or the fact that I am aware of it, is both motive and reason for the *epoché*. Or I do not believe the news because it is unpleasant. Here this fact is my motive, whereas the reason may be the same as before; but it is also possible that my behaviour lacks any objective reason. Where motive and reason are identical, the motivation will be reasonable. Where they differ, or where there is no reason at all, the attitude, or the behaviour concerning it, is unreasonable or unintelligible.

It should be noted that in the sphere of cognizance and attitudes the motive is never divorced from reasonable causes, since it is beyond reason and unreason. (Where one experience is called forth by another without its being possible to describe it as *caused*—such as the 'inclination'—we will speak of a stimulus, distinguishing it from the specifically reasonable motive). Every motive in this sense serves as a cause for a reasonable attitude of the subject. But it may be that the subject makes a slip in its behaviour. It will then do something different from what is demanded by the ruling motive, and what it actually does has its sufficient reason in a factual situation of which it is not aware. In our example the untrustworthiness of the messenger is a reasonable motive of the *epoché;* the behaviour, however, that would be demanded by the unpleasantness of the news, would be a defensive measure against what has been announced. The *epoché* intrudes here as a substitute of a rational refusal. Such a 'slip' in the behaviour, a division between motive and cause, occurs especially if the motivation has not been made explicitly, and can be revealed by explication. Hence the implication is a source of deception and error, and the explication is the means by which the rule of reason may be assured. Yet even 'unreasonable' motivations are possible only in the domain of reason, they are to be regarded as 'slips' of it.

4. *Free Acts.*

If the taking up or refusal of an attitude are performed as independent experiences, we have 'free acts' in the genuine sense, that is acts in which the ego not only experiences, but appears as master of its experiences. It is characteristic of them that they can only be 'made' in the authentic sense (in the form of the *cagito* in Husserl's terminology, as arising from the 'central ego' according to Pfänder and Hildebrand). They do not first stir imperceptibly at the back of my mind in order gradually to take possession of me, but I have to produce them out of myself, striking, as it were, a mental blow.

There are many kinds of such acts. "Assertion" is closely related to the acceptance of belief in a fact, though not identical with it; but it presupposes it and hence has to be clearly distinguished from it. I read the news that peace has been made. While taking cognizance of it I come to believe it, I assent to this belief, and on this basis I can now assert that peace has been made. Evidently this assertion is something new, not only with regard to the belief ('conviction'), but also to the acceptance of the belief. Conviction and assertion are attitudes to a fact, acceptance is an attitude to conviction. This, however, does not yet characterize it sufficiently. There is a kind of behaviour towards a fact correlative to its acceptance, which is different from the latter as well as from the assertion. This is recognition. I do not accept the belief; this means also: I deny the fact my recognition, I do not 'posit' its existence. (This recognition and its opposite, rejection, is, of course, not to be mistaken for the 'valuating' attitude of approval and disapproval, which may be directed to the fact as well as to belief in it, its acceptance and its recognition). As has been said, recognition, too, precedes assertion. I may be convinced of, and give my recognition to, many things without asserting them. By claiming that an assertion presupposes acceptance and recognition, we do not mean to say that it must be performed as a separate act. It is sufficient if it exists as the immanent character of the belief, if we take our stand on the conviction. As long as we fail to do this, we shall not make the assertion in question. For example, I may be convinced of the contents of a Reuter message. But I have the 'principle' not to believe Reuter messages, hence I shall not repeat it as an established fact, I shall not assert it. It is true, this statement is open to objection. People assert so much without sufficient evidence. Besides, assertions are not only made in good faith, there are also lies. Now here we must be careful. It goes without saying that there are assertions without sufficient evidence. In these cases they are founded on, or motivated by a conviction, the motives of which are not identical with their objective reasons, but which are nevertheless accepted or assumed. I am, for example, convinced of a Reuter message, I acknowledge and repeat it, because it is favourable, though I am not unaware of its unreliability. Though insufficiently founded, this may certainly be a genuine assertion. This is to be distinguished from cases in which I 'assert' something without being convinced of it. For example, I assure a sick person that he will soon be better, though I do not believe it (but without believing the contrary either). The motive of this assertion is my desire to calm the patient. It is without a foundation, or rather without an intellectual foundation. For 'assertion' here has two meanings: the theoretical one of stating a fact, and the practical one of inducing another person to believe this fact. The intellectual or theoretical foundation, i.e. belief in the fact, is lacking; but in its practical meaning the assertion is well founded, because of its motive, viz. my desire to calm the patient; and this, too, is of course a reasonable foundation.

Nevertheless, it seems to me not permissible to speak here of a genuine assertion. In making an assertion I posit, so to speak, an absolute state of affairs, at the same time placing it visibly before myself and others. This is possible only on the grounds of an assumed conviction. In giving an assurance without myself believing in it, I place the fact, so to speak, only before the other person, not before myself, and not as something absolute. By this we have not yet described a lie. This exists only if one believes the opposite of what one affirms to another person. We need hardly explain that in this case there is no genuine but a pseudo-assertion which, of course, has to be clearly distinguished from a false assertion. Hence we have to distinguish: (1) genuine assertions (based on conviction); they may be more or less well-founded, right or wrong; (2) assurances (without conviction) (3) lies (contradicting conviction).

We have not yet included the case of a conviction that is not accepted. Evidently this cannot be the motive of a genuine assertion. For in this case the fact is denied precisely that recognition which it needs in order to be posited absolutely. It seems to be possible to present the non-recognized fact in the same way as an 'assurance'. I may pass on a piece of news without reservations, though interiorly I still hesitate to assent to it. On closer examination, however, we shall yet notice a difference. I can give an assurance quite candidly and with a good conscience, though I do not believe in it, if I am not at all conscious of not believing in my words. But when I state something that I refuse to recognize, there is a felt opposition between my own interior attitude to the fact and its expression. I do it, so to speak, with a bad conscience (in our case an intellectual conscience), and that approaches it to a lie, though, of course, it is no lie.

All these cases of 'assuming' and 'refusing' an attitude, or recognizing or rejecting a fact, of assertions, assurances and lies, are concerned with free acts which the ego performs on its own account, but which it may just as well not perform. We have seen that they, like the attitudes, have their motives, and possibly causes that do not coincide with the motives. But the existence of the motives does not *compel* the ego to perform these acts. They do not, like the attitudes, appear simply by reason of their motives. The ego may have and recognize the motives and yet not perform the acts. I know for example that I could comfort the sick person with the assurance of his quick recovery which he hopes me to give him, I myself should like to help him, hence the motive is there; yet I fail to give him the assurance. One objection springs to mind: the omission, too, needs a motive; in other words, there are counter-motives. Perhaps I have the principle never to say anything of which I am not convinced; this would oppose my giving the desired assurance. This, surely, will often be the case. Yet if I am thus struggling with opposing motives, if I am confronted with making a decision, it is nevertheless once more I who make the decision. It does not come automatically as the tongue of the scales points to the side of the 'weightier' motive, but I decide *because* it is weightier. Even though more may be in favour of doing than of omitting something, the doing, too, needs the consent of my *fiat*. I may give it according to the 'weightiness' of the motives, but I can also give it without weighing them, and finally even if I consider the motives to carry equal weight. Hence free acts presuppose a motive; but apart from that they need an impulse which itself is not motivated.

With these considerations we have already approached the sphere of willing and acting. Yet it is absolutely necessary to distinguish the actual willing and acting from our free, or, as we may also call them, our 'voluntary' acts which comprise it. We may take as our point of departure the analysis of willing given by D. von Hildebrand in his *Idea of Moral Action* (Husserl-Jahrbuch vol. 3, 1916). He first distinguishes several notions of willing* that are often mixed up in ordinary speech: (1) striving *(das Sichbemühen)* e.g. I want to be good or to forgive, a willing that is quite compatible with being unable to

---

* German uses the one word *wollen* for such different English equivalents as willing, wanting, wishing, desiring etc.   Ed.

do something. (2) The purpose of doing something, e.g. I will go for a walk, a willing that necessarily presupposes a being able. (3) The will that is directed towards realizing a state of affairs (*Sachverhalt*). This is as different from the willing that is directed towards merely doing something as the action, i.e. the realizing of a state of affairs, is different from the activity in which no more than a condition of the subject is realized. This is again split up into the attitude of the will, the purpose of the will, and the actual introduction of the action. As regards willing in the first sense, we see that it is, indeed, a free act, but a special kind of it which is clearly distinguished from others, e.g. from asserting. Here we would only note that it is always concerned with a 'willing' subject's own behaviour, which is by no means the case for all free acts; but it is distinguished from other free acts that are also concerned with one's own behaviour (such as deciding, making a resolution, etc.) by not considering whether or not the subject is capable of the relevant behaviour.

If we now consider the act of purposing (sc. one's own action) we see that it has evidently to do with the free acts rather than being itself a free act. We cannot say that every free act *is* a purpose, nor would it be correct to assert that every free act presupposes one; but every free act *may* result from a purpose, the free acts define the sphere of subjective behaviour to which a purpose can be directed. They are the 'doing' of the subject which is the aim of the purpose. (We do not agree with Hildebrand in that he thinks it essential for the doing to include a behaviour of the body, *loc. cit.* p. 152). We think it absolutely necessary to speak also of purely intellectual and spiritual doing, nor would we restrict the action to a realization of facts in the external world. Whereas I may, indeed, strive for taking cognizance and defining attitudes, I need never strive for free acts, but can purpose them without further effort. The free acts may also be called voluntary with regard to just this conception of the will.

In contrast with the purpose, the attitude of the will, being a true attitude, is not a free act. We may strive for it (e.g. "really wanting to" do a good deed) but we cannot have the purpose. But we can once more purpose the purpose as a free act. On the other hand, it must be emphasized that every purpose, like every free act, presupposes an attitude, though not always an unequivocally defined one. A mere ideal, a knowledge or a taking cognizance of the action to which the free act is directed, does not suffice for its being performed. We have seen that in order to be able to assert something I must be convinced of it. In order to assure someone of a thing, I need not be convinced of the contents of the assurance, but I must somehow be 'interested' in the assurance itself. If I am to purpose something, I must take up an attitude of the will towards the thing I purpose, be it my own doing or the state of affairs I want to realize. But it should be stressed that the attitude which is demanded as the foundation of the free act need not be a 'living' one, it need not actually exist. It is sufficient if I recognize an attitude as demanded by reason and accept it, without its actually appearing.

If, finally, we consider the introduction of the action (or of the mere doing), the *fiat* by which it is started, we realize that this belongs necessarily to all genuine (including intellectual) doing, as an interior 'jerk' from which it starts its course. This need not be a special act, though this, too, is possible. I intend e.g. to tell somebody an important piece of news when a suitable opportunity arises. I am together with him, and in the course of the conversation there is a favourable moment. As soon as this is clear to me I say interiorly: 'Now' and begin my tale. Saying 'now' does not mean that I am renewing my purpose, with which I have been 'bursting' the whole time; but it is the 'fiat' that causes the transition from the purpose to its execution. How this 'fiat' is distinguished as a characteristic moment of the beginning action (instead of as a separate act) can perhaps best be seen in cases where an action arises immediately from the attitude of the will, without the mediation of a purpose. E.g. I see a man lifting his arm to strike another, and I stop the blow. From the attitude "This must not happen" the action follows immediately. There is no trace of a purpose, even the interior preparation expressed by the 'now' is lacking. Nevertheless, the 'jerk' which starts the action is still noticeable. We even find it in the 'compulsory' *(genötigt)* acts, as Reinach has called them, which lack a purpose as well as an attitude of the will. If someone forces me by threats to give up something, I do not at all *will* this giving up (in the sense of an attitude). I even reject it interiorly, nor do I purpose to make this sacrifice (though this is possible in some forms of compulsion), and yet I do it and introduce this doing by an interior jerk. We must here distinguish several possibilities. (1) There is in me no attitude of the will embracing the renunciation, but a (negative) one towards what is threatening me, and, recognizing the renunciation as a means for removing the threat, I decide on, and perform it. Here we still have a free act and no real compulsion. (2) I am completely under the influence of fear and consequently ready to do whatever is demanded of me. Here there can no longer be a question of an attitude of the will and of a purpose. We are confronted with a peculiar surrender of one's spontaneity, and in its place with a submission to another which as such is still to be regarded as understandable and motivated, but within the context of which the activity is no longer directed by motives. Besides, there are conditions which can be clarified only by a special analysis of the relations of subjects to each other. In our context we would like to say only this much: Insofar as the ego can still be considered the central point from which the enforced acts radiate, and has not sunk so low as to be a blind tool of another's will, the jerk that introduces all doing is still noticeable; in the other case we can no longer speak of a 'doing'. Hence the sphere of free acts which we equate with the doing of the ego may be defined by saying that they, and only they, *can* emerge from a purpose and *must* be introduced by a *fiat*.

Here we should like to consider briefly one class of free acts which we have met sometimes before, because a misunderstanding on this point might easily arise. An assurance, a renunciation of a claim, further also a granting, a refusal, a pardon, etc. are 'social acts' (according to Reinach), since they are also directed towards another subject. They may appear in the form of a communication in words, but they themselves are to be distinguished from it. The assertion must certainly be distinguished from its linguistic form. This can be seen even from the fact that the same linguistic expression may contain an assertion, an assurance, and a lie. In the same way the act of pardon or of refusal is distinguished from its communication to the person to whom it is addressed. On the other hand, the aforementioned acts may not be identified with the attitudes on which they are based. An interior attitude of forgiving, of granting and the like, corresponds to the attitude of the will which appears quite spontaneously if faced with a fact. This interior attitude appears equally spontaneously and is not arbitrary; it is the foundation on which the actual act of pardoning, granting etc. can or cannot be performed. It is possible that these free acts are performed though the corresponding attitudes have not appeared (as a purpose may be established without the will taking up an attitude to the facts), but in this case a peculiar void and spuriousness is attached to them, so that they are distinguished from the full and genuine pardon as an assurance is from a genuine assertion.

It is evident that in the sphere of free acts motivation (as distinct from the larger concept which we discussed in the beginning) gain a special significance. With regard to this we can understand it if Pfaender (*Motives and Motivations*, 1911, p. 183) would consider motivation as "only the peculiar relationship that exists between a demanding ground of the will and the act of the will that is based on it". He thinks it is essential to this relationship that one 'listens to' a fact that has been perceived, recognized, or been made conscious in some other way, that a demand proceeding from it has been perceived, recognized and possibly approved, and that the willing is founded on this demand. Such a demand (a *possible* ground for the will) becomes a real ground of the will and hence a motive only if the ego "founds the act of its will on the demand and educes it from it . . . the ego has no longer left the demand standing outside itself, but has let it enter itself, embodied it, and has then, supporting itself on it, performed the act of the will in agreement with the demand and thus, for the time being, fulfilled it ideally". He further emphasizes that it is characteristic of the act of the will (in contrast with the striving) that it is not 'blind in itself' but contains "in its being a consciousness of what is willed, that in it "opining, a practical primary thesis is posited" *(meinend ein praktischer Ursatz gesetzt wird);* finally, that it contains a spontaneity that is lacking in the striving; that it arises from the centre of the ego, but not as a happening, but as a peculiar doing, in that the centre of the ego carries out a spiritual blow centrifugally away from itself.

This description of willing may well be accepted, but we must realize that here the act of the will means the concrete unity of the attitude of the will as well as the purpose, and the definitions gained are shared between the two, but do not hold good for both in the same sense. Further, the description (if we disregard for the moment the limitation against the striving, and only consider the willing in its relation to motivation) holds good not only for the act of the will in its proper sense, but also for all other voluntary acts. If I forgive someone an insult because he feels regret, I first perceive only the regret, but do not leave it at that, and take up that attitude of a spiritual 'listening' in its regard of which Pfaender speaks. And now I perceive the demand of forgiving that arises from it, approve of it, finally grant it entrance, and perform, "supporting myself on it" the act of forgiving. (We would here, conformably with our previous statements, still distinguish: on the ground of the admitted demand the inner attitude of pardon appears, and the pardon is actually given). Thus the pardoning, in its whole structure, must be taken as a parallel to the act of the will. It is not at all to be interpreted in such a way that the will to forgive arises at once from the demand. This may be the case, but it is not at all necessary. But the motivation in that special sense which Pfaender visualizes should not be limited to the actual act of the will, but ought to be extended to the whole sphere of voluntary acts.

From FINITE AND ETERNAL BEING

Section III. *Life of the Mind and Motivation*

1. Two Modes of Being.

The certainty of one's own being is in a certain sense the primary form of cognition; not, indeed, the first in time, for the 'natural attitude' of man is to turn above all to the external world, and it takes him long to find himself; nor, again, in the sense of a principle, from which all other truth could be logically derived; but in the sense of being what is nearest to me, inseparable from me, and hence a point of departure behind which one cannot go. This certainty of being is an 'unreflected' certainty, i.e. it precedes all 'reflective' though, by which the mind leaves the original attitude of its life that had been turned to the objects, in order to look at itself. If the mind in such a reflexion becomes absorbed in the simple fact of its being, this will become a threefold question: What is the being of which I am aware? What is the ego that is aware of its being? What is the intellectual movement in which I am conscious of myself and of this movement? If I turn towards the being it shows in itself a twofold aspect: that of being and of non-being. The 'I am' cannot sustain the glance. That 'in which I am' is always another, and since the being and the intellectual movement are not separated, since I am 'in it', the being, too, is always another. The being of 'before now' is past and has made place for the being of 'now'. The being of which I am aware as my being, cannot be separated from transitoriness. Since it is 'actual' being —that is present and real—it is 'punctual' in the sense 'of a point' that is a 'now' between a 'no longer' and a 'not yet'. But while fluctuating, it is split into being and non-being, the idea of pure being is being revealed to us, the being that has no 'non-being' in itself, in which there is neither a 'no longer' nor a 'not yet', which is not temporal but eternal.

2. *The Human Being as Somatic, Psychic and Spiritual.*
Peculiarity of the Human Intellectual and Spiritual Life.

Man's being is a somatic-psychic-spiritual being. Insofar as
man's essence is spirit, he goes out of himself in his spiritual life
and enters a world that opens up to him without leaving himself.
Like every truly formed thing *(Gebilde)* he not only exhales his
essence spiritually, unconsciously expressing himself, he is, moreover, active in a personal and spiritual way. The human soul as
spirit elevates itself in its spiritual and intellectual life above
itself. But the human spirit is conditioned from above and from
below. It is embedded in the material thing which it animates
and forms into its bodily shape. The human person bears and
embraces his body and his soul, but he is at the same time borne
and embraced by them. His spirit life rises from a dark ground,
it ascends like the flame of a candle that shines, but is nourished
by a material that is not itself shining. And it shines without
being itself light all through: the human spirit is visible, but
not completely transparent to itself; it is able to enlighten, but
not completely to penetrate other things. We have already come
to know its darknesses: by its own inner light it knows indeed
its present life and much that once was its present life: but the
past is full of gaps, the future can be foreseen only in certain
details and with some probability, far more is indefinite and
uncertain, even though it can be apprehended in this indefinite-
ness and uncertainty. Origin and goal are completely inaccessible,
as long as we confine ourselves to the consciousness that belongs
to life itself and are not assisted by the experience of others, by
judging and concluding thought and by the truths of faith—all
of them aids which the pure spirit does not need for its own
self-knowledge. And the immediately certain life of the present
is the transitory fulfilment of a moment, at once sinking back
and soon slipping away altogether. The whole conscious life is
not equivalent to 'my being', it resembles the light surface above
a dark depth which is revealed in this surface. If we would
understand the fact that man is a person, we must try to
penetrate into this dark depth.

WORKS OF EDITH STEIN

(Those marked with an * are reproduced either wholly or in part in this anthology).

Edith Stein's *Werke* vols. 1—3, 1950ff. Nauwelaerts (Louvain) and Herder (Freiburg) ed. by Dr. Lucie Gelber and Fr. Romaeus Leuven, O.D.C., containing

*Kreuzeswissenschaft** (vol. 1)

*Endliches und Ewiges Sein** (vol. 2)

Des hl. Thomas von Aquino Untersuchungen über die Wahrheit (vols. 3—4).

*Frauenbildung und Frauenberufe,** Schnell & Steiner, München, 1949.

*Beiträge zur philosophischen Begründung der Psychologie und der Geisteswissenschaften,** Jahrbuch für Philosophie und phänomenologische Forschung, 5 vol., Halle a.d.S. 1922.

Eine Untersuchung über den Staat, ibid., 1925.

Husserls Phänomenologie und die Philosophie des hl. Thomas, Husserl-Festschrift, Halle a.d.S., 1929.

*Das Gebet der Kirche,** Bonifacius-Druckerei, Paderborn, n.d.

*Das Weihnachtsgeheimnis,** Karmel Maria vom Frieden, Köln, 1950.

Teresia von Jesus, Kanisius-Verlag, Konstanz, 2. ed., 1952.

Margareta Redi, Rita-Verlag, Würzburg, 1934.

Der Intellekt und die Intellektuellen, in *"Das heilige Feuer"*, Juli-August, 1931.

Ways to Know God,* in "The Thomist", July 1946, Baltimore.

Natur und Übernatur in Goethes Faust, MS, Edith Stein-Archives, Louvain.

Die Bestimmung der Frau, MS, ibid.

Der Eigenwert der Frau in seiner Bedeutung für das Leben des Volkes, MS, ibid.

Ein auserwähltes Gefäss der göttlichen Weisheit, MS, ibid.

INDEX